Global Education
Using Technology to Bring the World to Your Students

Laurence Peters

International Society for Technology in Education
EUGENE, OREGON • WASHINGTON, DC

Global Education
Using Technology to Bring the World to Your Students
Laurence Peters

© 2009 International Society for Technology in Education

World rights reserved. No part of this book may be reproduced or transmitted in any form or by any means—electronic, mechanical, photocopying, recording, or by any information storage or retrieval system—without prior written permission from the publisher. Contact Permissions Editor, ISTE, 180 West 8th Ave, Suite 300, Eugene, OR 97401-2916; fax: 1.541.302.3780; e-mail: permissions@iste.org or visit www.iste.org/permissions/.

Director of Book Publishing: *Courtney Burkholder*
Acquisitions Editor: *Jeff V. Bolkan*
Production Editors: *Lanier Brandau, Lynda Gansel*
Production Coordinator: *Rachel Bannister*
Graphic Designer: *Signe Landin*
Copy Editor: *Kathy Hamman*
Indexer: *Seth Maislin*
Cover Design, Book Design and Production: *Gwen Thomsen Rhoads*

Library of Congress Cataloging-in-Publication Data

Peters, Laurence, 1952-
  Global education : using technology to bring the world to your students / Laurence Peters. — 1st ed.
    p. cm.
  Includes bibliographical references and index.
  ISBN 978-1-56484-258-9
  1. International education—Computer networks. 2. Internet in education.
  I. International Society for Technology in Education. II. Title.
  LC1090.P45 2009
  370.116078'54678—dc22
                                            2009004802

First Edition
ISBN: 978-1-56484-258-9

Printed in the United States of America

International Society for Technology in Education (ISTE)
Washington, DC, Office:
    1710 Rhode Island Ave. NW, Suite 900, Washington, DC 20036-3132
Eugene, Oregon, Office:
    180 West 8th Ave, Suite 300, Eugene, OR 97401-2916
Order Desk: 1.800.336.5191
Order Fax: 1.541.302.3778
Customer Service: orders@iste.org
Book Publishing: books@iste.org
Book Sales and Marketing: booksmarketing@iste.org
Rights and Permissions: permissions@iste.org
Web: www.iste.org

Photos: ©iStockphoto.com
Cover (left to right): Yuri Arcurs, Quavondo, Katya Monakhova, bonniej; Background: Beholding Eye.
Text: Chapter 1, Yuri Arcurs; Chapter 2, Rob Friedman; Chapter 3, Quavondo; Chapter 4, Bonnie Jacobs; Chapter 5, Katya Monakhova; Chapter 6, Elena Elisseeva; Chapter 7, Bonnie Jacobs; Chapter 8, Tatiana Belova; Chapter 9, Chris Schmidt.

About ISTE

The International Society for Technology in Education (ISTE) is the trusted source for professional development, knowledge generation, advocacy, and leadership for innovation. A nonprofit membership association, ISTE provides leadership and service to improve teaching, learning, and school leadership by advancing the effective use of technology in PK–12 and teacher education.

Home of the National Educational Technology Standards (NETS), the Center for Applied Research in Educational Technology (CARET), and ISTE's annual conference and exposition (formerly known as the National Educational Computing Conference, or NECC), ISTE represents more than 100,000 professionals worldwide. We support our members with information, networking opportunities, and guidance as they face the challenge of transforming education. To find out more about these and other ISTE initiatives, visit our website at **www.iste.org**.

As part of our mission, ISTE Book Publishing works with experienced educators to develop and produce practical resources for classroom teachers, teacher educators, and technology leaders. Every manuscript we select for publication is carefully peer-reviewed and professionally edited. We value your feedback on this book and other ISTE products. E-mail us at **books@iste.org**.

About the Author

Laurence Peters grew up in London, England, and attended the University of Sussex, where he later qualified as an English teacher before gaining a master's degree in English and education at the University of London. He became a teaching fellow at the University of Michigan, earning his doctorate in English and education. He later became interested in issues related to education policy and pursued a law degree, which led to senior positions with the U.S. government, first as counsel to a House of Representatives education subcommittee, then senior positions with the U.S. Department of Education (1993–2001).

After leaving the federal government, Peters directed the Mid-Atlantic Regional Technology in Education Consortium (MARTEC) based at Temple University in Philadelphia. His career-long interest has been in developing and implementing programs that can assist the educationally disadvantaged. He co-wrote *From Digital Divide to Digital Opportunity*, published by Scarecrow Press in 2003, and co-edited a book with Chris Dede, *Scaling Up Success: Lessons from Technology-Based Educational Improvement*. Peters teaches a graduate-level course on the Integration of Global Perspectives for the University of Maryland University College (UMUC). He is married with three children and lives in Rockville, Maryland.

Acknowledgment

I have a lot of people to thank for this book, one person in particular: Dr. Katherine Woodward, Director of the master's degree in instructional education program at University of Maryland University College (UMUC), deserves some special credit for encouraging me to pursue this project and for her determination to make the integration of global perspectives an integral part of the program she directs at UMUC. Thanks also to Dr. Edwin H. Gragert, US iEARN coordinator, who provided many insights and offered his time and encouragement, and to Yvonne Marie Andres, President of Global SchoolNet Foundation's *Global Schoolhouse*, and her superb group of global educator awardees, many of whose great insights are included in this book.

Dedication

To my mother, Deborah Peters, who continues to inspire me with her global vision, and for my children, Noah, Jonathan, and Emma, who I hope will inherit and work toward a more harmonious world.

Contents

Introduction — 1

Why I Wrote This Book 3

Global Education and 9/11 4

Shifting Definitions of Global Education 5

How to Use This Book 6

1 Global Education and the Web 2.0 Revolution — 9

The Web 2.0 Revolution and Learning Theory 10

HISTORICAL INTERLUDE—The Origins of Global Education 12

Getting Started Is Easier Than You Think 13

Global Learning and Curriculum Objectives 14

HISTORICAL INTERLUDE—Erasmus and Comenius 16

Security Concerns 17

2 Pathways to Global Education — 21

Pathway: Empathy for Others 22

Pathway: Finding New Ways to Enrich and Engage 23

CASE STUDY—Marsha Goren's Journey as a Globaldreamer 24

CASE STUDY—Early Experiences on the Path to Becoming a Global Educator 25

Pathway: Desire for Social Justice 27

HISTORICAL INTERLUDE—Opposing Viewpoints: John Dewey and Ellwood P. Cubberley 28

Support and Mentoring 29

CASE STUDY—The Power of Mentoring and Collaboration 31

Collaboration and Lesson Planning 33

HISTORICAL INTERLUDE—Mid- to Late Twentieth Century 34

Accountability Pressures. 36

3 The Flat Classroom Project — 39

What Is the Flat Classroom Project? 39

Blogging's Role 40

Podcasts and Vodcasts. 41

Skype and Similar Tools 41

Classroom Ning 42

Aligning Project Purpose, Learning Objective, Content,
and the NETS with Product Outcome 43

Preparing Students to Launch a Global Classroom 49

The Flat Classroom Project Inspires Others. 50

4 iEARN — 55

HISTORICAL INTERLUDE—Célestin Freinet. 57

The Founding of iEARN 59

iEARN Expands 60

iEARN Project: De Orilla a Orilla 62

iEARN Project: Feeding Minds Fighting Hunger. 63

Evaluating iEARN 63

5 Global Schoolhouse and Other Global Education Networks   67

Global Schoolhouse 67

ePals 70

CASE STUDY—Interview with Accomplished Global Educator
Kim Cofino 72

Many Other Opportunities Await! 76

6 Connecting Global Themes to Your Curriculum   81

Robert Hanvey's Foundational Essay 81

Preparation Is Essential...................................... 85

Sample Module Design 87

7 Quick Ways to Get Started   91

An ePals Activity for Elementary Students 91

A Virtual Tour Guide Activity for Middle School Students 93

Engaging Middle and High School Students
with Current Events 93

Connecting Middle and High School Students
with Their Passions... 95

8 Final Thoughts   97

9 Sample Lesson Plans — 103

Cinderella Around the World 103

Do Food Choices Affect Global Warming? 107

Cross-Cultural Pen Pals 115

Appendix A: Glossary 119

Appendix B: Web Resources 125

Appendix C: National Educational Technology Standards 139

Appendix D: References 149

Index 157

Introduction

Eleventh-grade students in Bangladesh exchange video interviews with tenth-grade counterparts in Georgia. They are discussing issues concerning globalization from Tom Friedman's bestselling book *The World Is Flat*. Their teachers, Vicki Davis and Julie Lindsay, planned for six weeks to create what is now the award-winning Flat Classroom Project. The students, separated by 8,500 miles and 11 time zones, were required to analyze the way the world has changed following the advent of the world wide web. They used **podcasts**, **wikis**, **RSS feeds**, and **videoconferencing** to collaborate. They interviewed world experts using multimedia presentation tools and were honored by a panel of international judges as a result of what has been dubbed a "reflection interview" via podcast (http://flatclassroom.podomatic.com/entry/2007-01-20T06_07_55-08_00).

A science teacher and a moral education teacher in French-speaking Québec launched a worldwide seminar and fund-raiser based on their discussion of poverty and HIV/AIDS between students in a Ugandan orphanage and students around the world. The project, "Survivor Gault," involved 30 hours of **videoconference** communications (and other technologies) addressing the problems of the 70% of the earth's population who live on less than $1 a day. Much of the information had been gleaned by the students from the people in the Ugandan community.

Students in Evanston Township in Illinois learn Japanese, Hebrew, Latin, Spanish, French, and German using online discussions with counterparts from around the globe. They attend school clubs such as the Model United Nations and clubs devoted to Islamic Culture, Tea Ceremony, and Amnesty International as part of their efforts to learn about other cultures.

These projects and others like them win awards and catch headlines, but unfortunately they are far from mainstream. In today's educational landscape, that's a pity. More than one in four of California's residents was born outside the United States. Students there speak more than 60 languages, and yet most of these classrooms, like classrooms throughout the country, remain **monocultural**. One rural school district in Arkansas registers over 2,000 ESL students speaking 16 different languages. New York City is home to students representing every country in the world.

In the United States, the percentage of foreign-born residents rose from 9.7% to 28.4% between 1960 and 2000, shifting the population as a whole from predominantly

European to Latin American and Asian. This increased diversity has affected most Western European countries and cities. In the United States, more than 1 million new immigrants arrive every year. Yet most U.S. classrooms remain resolutely monocultural.

The skills that students learned while participating in the projects mentioned above are important to fostering an understanding about their own culture and its relationship to other cultures. Those projects also provide models of technology integration and can help foster a new kind of global awareness, an awareness stimulated when students connect and collaborate with students and experts in other countries and on other continents.

Howard Gardner is a distinguished professor at the Harvard Graduate School of Education. His theory of multiple intelligences points to one potential reason why many of today's students have a poor grasp of the world around them. He suggests that students may not be retaining geographical knowledge because schools favor teaching it in the abstract—teaching mainly to two kinds of intelligences (the linguistic and logical-mathematical) to the detriment of others, including the interpersonal (the ability to empathize with others and see the world from another's viewpoint). Teachers might do more to provide a greater range of opportunities for students to exercise their interpersonal intelligence by using digital technologies to connect students across geographical boundaries, expanding their interest and curiosity about the world in a deeper way than can be stimulated by a textbook.

Gardner was one of the first to point out the need for schools and their students to catch up with the new globalizing forces that require young people to graduate with the great range of social and cultural skills necessary to problem solve and collaborate across the world. One might wonder: Why are schools so slow to pay attention to these new realities? According to *National Geographic* and *Roper Public Affairs* surveys, U.S. public school students remain woefully undereducated about the world and its people. A 2006 survey reports that in the United States:

- Seventy-four percent of students believe that English is the primary language spoken by most people in the world, rather than Mandarin Chinese.
- Fewer than three in ten of those surveyed think it is absolutely necessary to know where countries are located.
- Only 14% believe that speaking another language fluently is a necessary skill.
- More than 80% could not locate Afghanistan or Iraq on a map of the Middle East and Asia.

Why I Wrote This Book

I want to share how emerging and established web-based technologies can allow students to view the world from a **global perspective** in ways never before possible.

I came to the United States from England when I was in my twenties. Like so many international visitors who had come before me, I appreciated the excitement, energy, and new opportunities that opened up for me after I enrolled at an American graduate school. Later, when I started teaching in the United States, first at the high school and later at the college level, students were eager to have my British perspective. I enjoyed breaking through their stereotypes of England as largely being populated by mansions and upper class people wearing tweeds and bowler hats. I had also begun to examine my own stereotypes of Americans and the United States—as a land of fast cars, swimming pools, and skyscrapers.

Global Education Fits All Subjects, All Grades

Kenneth and Barbara Tye asked teachers (11 elementary and secondary school faculties in an inservice professional development project they worked on between 1985 and 1989) what was meant by global education. "Large numbers thought global education was something for the social studies classes, or in the case of primary teachers, for the upper grades."

The Tyes' view was quite simple—rather than reserving global education for social studies, global perspectives (their preferred term) should be "taught in every subject and at every grade level. By using data from World Bank publications, the population reference bureau, or the 1990 census, for instance, math teachers helped students learn basic computational skills and at the same time, something about the world in which they live."

Besides visiting a place and living there for some time, how else might we acquire a deeper understanding of the place and its people? I had come to believe fervently that everyone should have a better grasp of how media stereotypes and oversimplifications cannot substitute for the reality of a place.

My answers came to me gradually after the Internet enabled practically everyone in the world with telephone service to be in contact. One did not need a passport to travel on the Internet—students could travel virtually from the comfort of their own classrooms. The possibilities became even more tantalizingly real with the advent of free videoconferencing and the initiation of a range of collaborative tools available with **web 2.0**. These tools allow us to see our own country through the lens of another, a sensation that may be akin to the feeling bilingual speakers feel when they interact with speakers of both their mother and adopted tongues. We only realize how deeply enveloped we are in our own culture when we have an opportunity to stand outside of it and look at it from a stranger's perspective.

The web-based tools available today have never been so user friendly—the personal connections formed when students use an application like ePals create a firsthand interest in another country and a fresh sensitivity to their own culture and country. Video- and audioconferencing provide new ways of connecting students worldwide. Specifically students' ability simply to send video or audio files adds a new dimension to the global exchange, sparking a new energy for learning and a curiosity unlikely to be matched by a traditional lesson. Students from different countries and backgrounds can learn to appreciate their differences and delight in their commonalities. The goal of creating a more diverse and tolerant multicultural classroom can be achieved through the power of real-life examples rather than a textbook-directed lesson.

Global Education and 9/11

No book on global education can ignore the huge impact of 9/11. There is evidence that despite the rhetoric from politicians and leading educators that followed the event—talk about rethinking the curriculum to develop a less nationalistic view of the world—most U.S. schools have not changed their predominately monocultural approach to teaching and learning.

We'll see that the tide is finally beginning to turn towards more global awareness in U.S. schools. More schools are creating **global academies**, and the International Baccalaureate exam now penetrates more high school curricula; the business community is more firmly behind the call for a change in the ways schools prepare students for new challenges posed by a global economy. We can use digital technology and the global connections it allows to demonstrate to our increasingly diverse student bodies that our world is multi-, not mono-, cultural. We can avoid the marginalization of minority cultures by reaching beyond food festivals and Flag Day celebrations and spending more thought on how to deeply integrate global perspectives into the curriculum. Instead of learning about the world in the abstract, students now have the opportunity to experience the world firsthand through the power of the Internet.

The Council of Chief State School Officers (CCSSO) in its "Global Education Policy Statement" of November 2006 listed several challenges. Among the recommendations were the following:

> CCSSO and its members believe that in order to address the challenges of the 21st century, our education system must reflect knowledge and understanding of global perspectives and dimensions as well as the multifaceted perspectives within our own country; therefore, we believe certain core areas must be addressed in order for American students to thrive in and contribute to the global society. Our students must learn about many cultures as an integrated part of their study of literature, history, social studies, natural sciences, the arts, and other courses throughout the curriculum. Only by learning about other cultures, faiths, and ways of living will they be able to better their understanding of the various perspectives that frame our world and the people who inhabit it. More than ever before, students from around the globe are learning to adapt to change and to capitalize on expanding opportunities to become multilingual and learn to use mathematics, science, and technological skills in ways that meet or exceed the levels of current American students. We must take a constructive, positive, and innovative approach to preparing our children in a similar fashion, increasing the rigor of our academic standards, and thereby ensuring that all students are prepared to succeed in a global society.

Shifting Definitions of Global Education

What do we mean when we use the phrase "global education"?

There are many definitions of **global education**. Some blend ideas from international education (a focus on international relations), peace studies (incorporating ideas from conflict resolution), and social studies (an emphasis on history, civics, and geographical themes). I prefer to think of global education as experienced educator Sara Coumantarakis does—by thinking of the educational goals that we share when we apply the concept to our teaching.

Presented on the Defining Global Education webpage (http://imminentshift.com/global/define.html), Coumantarakis defines global education as teaching and learning with a global perspective:

- Recognizing the interdependencies and interconnections of issues, regions, peoples, places, systems, and times;

- Infusing global issues, such as sustainable development, environmental care, peace, and human rights, into traditional subject areas;

- Working toward active, responsible global citizenship and building a more peaceful, just, and sustainable world.

Because this definition includes the idea that "**global perspectives**" or "**global awareness**" should be a component of every subject taught, including math and science, the natural question arises: How? Should the issues related to global awareness be considered add-ons, or should they be integrated into the curriculum?

A key reason for writing this book is my belief that a focused use of digital technologies can assist with infusing content standard for all subjects with vital topics related to global awareness, such as global warming, the energy crisis, terrorism, and HIV/AIDS, to name a few. Through the application of web 2.0 technologies, students can come closer to grasping the relevance of the "traditional curriculum" to today's global challenges by directly connecting with students who are facing the same issues through a different cultural lens.

Most of us agree that as the 21st century progresses, we are moving into a more globally integrated world—a world more interdependent and demanding of key skills like problem solving, collaborating with globally dispersed teams, and using technology effectively to do so.

How to Use This Book

This book will help you integrate global perspectives into your instruction using web-based technologies. Its purpose is to provide K–12 teachers and those involved in professional development a basis for understanding the inclusion of these perspectives. Specifically, the book is designed to show how adding a web-enabled global dimension to your students' classroom can enhance their understanding of content while giving them a new perspective on its relevance and deepening their awareness of global realities.

> **UNESCO Universal Declaration on Cultural Diversity**
>
> The UNESCO Universal Declaration on Cultural Diversity was adopted unanimously by the General Conference at its 31st session on November 2, 2001, less than two months after 9/11. Article 2 of that declaration gives strong support for pluralistic approaches to culture and identity:
>
>> In our increasingly diverse societies, it is essential to ensure harmonious interaction among people and groups with plural, varied and dynamic cultural identities as well as their willingness to live together. Policies for the inclusion and participation of all citizens are guarantees of social cohesion, the vitality of civil society and peace. Thus defined, cultural pluralism gives policy expression to the reality of cultural diversity. Indissociable from a democratic framework, cultural pluralism is conducive to cultural exchange and to the flourishing of creative capacities that sustain public life.
>
> *http://unesdoc.unesco.org/images/0012/001271/127160m.pdf*

The book is structured to help you find your own "global pathway," one that lets you connect subject matter content with a global dimension that makes sense in terms of relevant content standards and key pedagogical principles. This book will provide you with step-by-step guidelines for getting started or supporting what you are already doing. This book will also provide you with the following:

- A survey of global networks, such as iEARN and ePals, designed to facilitate global collaboration

- Guidance to support a successful lesson or module if you decide not to use a network such as the ones mentioned above

- An introduction to web 2.0 technologies (such as wikis and blogs) to support global awareness

- Resources you can use to get started, including lesson plans and useful websites

As we discuss how educators are integrating global learning through the use of web 2.0 tools, I include Historical Interludes that give you some grounding in and perspectives on the history of global education. Also included are overviews of instructional theories as they relate to distance and global learning and model lesson plans.

As you work your way through the book, you may find terms that are unfamiliar to you. The first time a potentially unfamiliar term is used in the text, you'll find it in bold, and it will be included in Appendix A: Glossary, in the back of the book. You'll find a listing of websites and their addresses in the back of the book under Appendix B: Web Resources. An active and updated list of the book's web resources is also available on the author's website (www.umuc.edu/globalk12).

You'll also find a rather extensive listing of additional resources in the Appendixes to help inform and guide your work in using web 2.0 and other Internet tools to bring global learning and awareness to your classrooms.

The sample lesson plans in Chapter 9 are designed to provide you with a starting point. Though each is created for use in specific subjects and for particular grade levels, the plans are basic enough for you to adapt and expand for your own purposes. You will also find a rich array of web resources that will help guide you in designing your own unique curriculum in this arena using any number of the tools and applications mentioned in this book.

A companion video to this book entitled "Creating a Global Difference: Conversations for 21st-Century Teachers" can be viewed by visiting the University of Maryland University College Master of Education in Instructional Technology program website, on the "Global Perspectives Resource" page (**www.umuc.edu/globalk12**) and clicking on the the link to the video's title.

The video is designed to be used in several ways. First, taken in its entirety, the video provides an introduction to the reasons we need to be using the world wide web to help today's students become more globally aware. Second, the video serves as an introduction to some of the leading global education networks, such as iEARN, Global Nomads, and Global Relief, and how those networks developed into their present configurations. Third, the interviews with expert educators from all the over the world can be used by teacher educators to examine more closely the rationales for integrating a global dimension into the classroom. You will find excerpts from the video within the content of the book. I suggest using the video to help educate colleagues and local decision makers about global learning.

1

Global Education and the Web 2.0 Revolution

Something important happened to the world wide web during the three-year period between the launch of MySpace in 2003 and YouTube in 2005. During the year that YouTube was created, a Pew Research study (Lenhart & Madden, 2005) found that 57% of young people in America were using computers for creative activities such as writing or mixing and constructing multimedia. Barely two years later, Pew Research (Lenhart & Madden, 2007) found that 55% of online teens had created a personal profile online and 55% had used **social networking sites**. During this period, the web moved from being an impersonal library of static text pages—produced by those with the resources to master the programming language—to an interactive multimedia social network available to all. Millions of young people were involved in this reinvention of the web. Many of these **digital natives** were likely your students. As a generation, they have made the web their own, investing their time and youthful energy in creating **digital identities** on social networking sites such as Facebook, MySpace, and LinkedIn.

> "The real revolution of technology is to help our students build relationships that extend our understanding of who they are on the planet."
>
> *Alan November*

The Web 2.0 Revolution and Learning Theory

This **web 2.0** revolution represents an important opportunity for educators to globalize their classrooms by taking advantage of students' built-in comfort level with these new tools. Web 2.0 provides an opportunity to break down barriers (whether they are social or ethnic) among far-flung students. As part of what might be called a historical convergence, the web 2.0 revolution coincides in an interesting way with recent developments in learning theory: we learn more effectively in group interactions than through classroom lectures (Downes, n.d.).

Web 2.0 makes possible online communities that offer exciting implications for the classroom. One of the most articulate spokesmen for this view is John Seeley Brown, visiting scholar and advisor to the provost at the University of Southern California and former chief scientist of Xerox and director of its Palo Alto Research Center. Brown suggests that the Internet's most profound impact on learning may be the socially-based learning opportunities (blogs, wikis, and social networking sites) it offers. Brown (2008) and his co-author offer the following definition of **social learning**: It is "…based on the premise that our understanding of content is socially constructed through conversations about that content and through grounded interactions, especially with others, around problems or actions. The focus is not so much on what we are learning but on how we are learning."

An important reason for the unique effectiveness of social learning, unlike traditional methodology, has to do with the fact that learners in such settings are never passive; social situations are always dynamic, demanding that students be alert as the conversation changes course and participants are forced to take on new roles of teacher, student, or skeptic. Seeley Brown is among a number of learning experts who have seen the seeds of a new kind of 21st-century schooling within the emerging web 2.0 technologies—a future in which neither the teacher nor the student are dependent upon a single textbook, classic text, or essay. While in traditional classrooms students need play only one role, that of passive recipient of information, students using web 2.0 technologies can play multiple roles, roles that demand they test out their knowledge and understanding of a topic in order to create a result the entire group can agree represents their best thinking. Whether that outcome is in the form of a wiki, a webpage, a video, podcast, or a slide presentation, the work depends on working together through multiple iterations. Figure 1.1 is a snapshot summary of web-2.0-enabled student development compared with the text-dominated method.

Web 2.0	Text-dominated
Multiple teachers/Student-centered	One-teacher-centered
Different topics for different students	One size fits all
Multiple products	One product
Multiple audiences	One audience (teacher)
Multiple media	Single-text-based
Collaborative	Competitive
Synchronous and **Asynchronous**	Synchronous
Flexible schedule	Inflexible schedule

FIGURE 1.1 Student development opportunities: Web 2.0 vs. Text-dominated

Positioned in the global context, web 2.0 offers an exceptional opportunity for teachers to provide their students with a grasp of collaborative problem solving. These same students are now being called upon to understand the cultural perspectives of students who come from differing social and ethnic backgrounds.

Web 2.0 developments have important implications for **global educators**. Because students have become accustomed to sharing multimedia materials (photos, video, and music), the challenge of breaking down cultural barriers that at one time might have impeded any kind of meaningful collaboration is now considerably eased. Additionally, web 2.0 provides no-cost avenues for students to connect with their peers, independent of any special service such as ePals or a global school network. Social networking sites like Google Groups, Facebook, and MySpace are easily accessible for anyone with access to the world wide web. Translation tools such as BabelFish help overcome language barriers and are ideal for the speed at which web 2.0 communications flow.

It's safe to say that all students, no matter what their skill levels, intelligences (visual, spatial, auditory), or interests, can use these tools to experience global communications and develop meaningful connections with worldwide counterparts.

HISTORICAL INTERLUDE

The Origins of Global Education

> If we cannot bring our own cultural context into perspective, then we cannot take the perspective of culturally-different others. And when we cannot take the perspective of others, we cannot imagine their reality. And if we do not imagine their reality, we cannot be competent in the intercultural communication demanded by multicultural societies and global intentionalities.
>
> *Milton Bennett (2001)*

Have you ever wondered why the phrase "citizen of the world" has such resonance? This idea, said to be first uttered by Diogenes in ancient Greece, was part of a worldview that the Stoic segment of Greek society believed was the way human beings should exist in the world. It was a radical thought back then because Greeks defined themselves as belonging to cities (the root of the word "citizen" is "city"). Diogenes broke new ground when answering the question, "Where do you come from?" He said, "I am a citizen of the world." He earned a following from those who believed that we all share a humanity deeper than could be described by a mere geographical location. The Stoics believed (as explicated by the classical scholar Martha Nussbaum) that we each dwell in two communities—the local community of our birth and the community of human argument—both of which are included in the term the Stoics coined, *kosmu polites*, or world citizen.

Martha Nussbaum (1994) wrote persuasively on these topics in her essay "Patriotism and Cosmopolitanism":

> The Stoics stress that to be a citizen of the world one does not need to give up local identifications, which can frequently be a source of great richness in life. They suggest that we think of ourselves not as devoid of local affiliations, but as surrounded by a series of concentric circles. The first one is drawn around the self; the next takes in one's immediate family; then follows the extended family; then, in order, one's neighbors or local group, one's fellow city-dwellers, one's fellow countrymen—and we can easily add to this list groupings based on ethnic, linguistic, historical, professional, gender, and sexual identities. Outside all these circles is the largest one, that of humanity as a whole. Our task as citizens of the world will be to "draw the circles somehow toward the center" (Stoic philosopher Hierocles, 2nd century CE), making all human beings more like our fellow city dwellers, and so on. In other words, we need not give up our special affections and

identifications, whether ethnic or gender-based or religious. We need not think of them as superficial, and we may think of our identity as in part constituted by them. We may and should devote special attention to them in education. But we should work to make all human beings part of our community of dialogue and concern, base our political deliberations on that interlocking commonality, and give the circle that defines our humanity a special attention and respect.

It is this community that is, most fundamentally, the source of our moral obligations. With respect to the most basic moral values such as justice, "we should regard all human beings as our fellow citizens and neighbors" (Plutarch, *On the Fortune of Alexander,* 1994). We should regard our deliberations as, first and foremost, deliberations about human problems of people in particular concrete situations, not problems growing out of a national identity that is altogether unlike that of others.

As Seneca memorably stated in *De Otio* (n.d.), it is the community of "human argument and aspiration" that "is truly great and truly common, in which we look neither to this corner nor to that, but measure the boundaries of our nation by the sun."

Getting Started Is Easier Than You Think

There are many reasons to offer your students a global perspective throughout the curriculum. Before the advent of web 2.0 technologies, we might have paid lip service to the notion that students need to become more globally literate, to understand how to work and problem solve with people from different cultures and points of view. But with today's technologies, students are able to connect with counterparts halfway around the globe, using voice, text, and video. For the first time teachers can, to paraphrase Alan November, truly provide students with the opportunity to build relationships that extend their own understanding of who they are on the planet.

Students can take advantage of advanced digital tools to complete a collaborative science project. They are able to analyze data collected at one geographic location and compare it with that collected at another location. Students can use their own media (photos, audio, or video interviews) to show their part of the world and share it with others. Students gain a full range of cultural understandings that can only come when individuals from two cultures are in close working contact. They are more inclined in these immediate settings to be curious about one another and the forces that have shaped each other's culture and beliefs.

A key advantage of utilizing web 2.0 tools in the classroom is that they provide students with the ability to create resources (typically a blog or wiki) that a teacher can easily integrate into a project and that support the students' ability to work independently. Blogs and wikis can provide a continuing flow of feedback in real time. Another advantage is students' ability to see at any one time all the various relevant project elements: the original assignment, other students' questions and answers, and so on. Student work can also be supported through the use of multimedia tools, assisting visually or aurally impaired learners. Podcasts, **vodcasts**, and narrated slide shows assist a variety of learning styles.

These tools also can help organize students' schedules. I particularly like 30Boxes (www.30boxes.com), a free shared calendar and group organizer tool. Special-needs students may benefit from closer teacher monitoring, special tutorial assistance, or templates that can ease the complexity of certain assignments. A tool like **Digital Storyteller** (www.digitalstoryteller.org) is a one-stop site where students can identify images (from sources like Flickr), construct a script, and create a voice narrative without much technical skill.

Global Learning and Curriculum Objectives

Although these ideas sound good, I bet some of you are thinking, "You don't really understand my classroom, my courses, and the way I have to cover a certain curriculum. People will start complaining if the test scores don't improve." This objection is serious—teachers everywhere have been overburdened with all kinds of demands and are wary of taking on any new responsibilities, particularly if the payoff may not be immediate in terms of test score increases. Providing students with a global perspective may also sound nice in theory, but some may counter that because the students are exposed to world history and social studies, enough resources are already available in this particular curriculum area.

I suggest that educators in almost every subject and grade level can simultaneously meet curriculum objectives and incorporate a global perspective. As we will see in a later chapter, global connections are embedded in most of the national and state standards for all the subject areas; they are not solely contained in the fields of world history, geography, and social studies.

Writing to an ePal partner, collaborating on a script to be used in a multimedia presentation, comparing and contrasting pollution levels of major rivers, or taking ocean temperatures at different latitudes are not distractions from the curriculum. These activities can serve as a way to generate higher levels of motivation and interest in subject areas through stimulating, hands-on involvement.

Another barrier facing integrating global perspectives into the curriculum is simple inertia in the face of what appears to be an overwhelming challenge. After all, the very term "global perspective" seems, by definition, to conjure up a large and unmanageable universe of topics to consider. So the natural question is: Where to begin?

Throughout this book, you'll find ways to make the connection as a global educator, to enrich your curriculum and motivate your students as they explore the world with web 2.0 technologies such as:

- Podcasts
- Wikis
- Blogs
- Media sharing sites such as Flickr and YouTube
- Videoconferencing
- Google documents
- **VoiceThread**
- **Vlogs**

These tools are easy to use. Dive in and experiment! Many of the terms and resources mentioned here can be found in Appendix A: Glossary and Appendix B: Web Resources. Kathy Shrock recently assembled a list of free web 2.0 tools for Discovery Education: http://school.discoveryeducation.com/schrockguide/edtools.html.

HISTORICAL INTERLUDE

Erasmus and Comenius

The Romans believed that to be fully educated, they needed to return to the intellectual world that the Greeks created. They adapted their gods and myths to fit Greek values. For six centuries, privileged Roman children learned Greek in school and admired Greek classical achievements across the Mediterranean. Not surprisingly perhaps, the rediscovery of classical wisdom in the 15th century was in part a rediscovery of Latin and Greek as the foundations of a common curriculum that stretched across the former Roman Empire.

This was an empire in danger of fragmenting, however, as religious wars heated up and nation states began to exercise their muscle in response to new alliances between Protestants and Catholics. It was left to religious leaders like Desiderius Erasmus (1466–1536), a Roman Catholic priest, to seek some measure of restraint as he reminded his many followers across Europe of the ideal of universalistic learning that grounded classical thought, even at a time when the Protestant and Catholic tensions were approaching boiling point.

Erasmus rejected the church's orthodox position that claimed religious learning as the only means to true wisdom. Drawing upon his deep reading of classical authors, he illustrated that wisdom is universal and not the property of one particular sect, religion, or nationality. His arguments were often couched in satirical terms—for example, this excerpt from the brilliant and witty *The Praise of Folly* (1509) mocks the pretensions of those who view their own national origins as some privileged view of wisdom:

> Nature has planted, not only in particular men but even in every nation, and scarce any city is there without it, a kind of common self-love. And hence is it that the English, besides other things, particularly challenge to themselves beauty, music, and feasting. The Scots are proud of their nobility, alliance to the crown, and logical subtleties. The French think themselves the only well-bred men. The Parisians, excluding all others, arrogate to themselves the only knowledge of divinity.... And, not to instance in every particular, you see, I conceive, how much satisfaction this Self-love, who has a sister also not unlike herself called Flattery, begets everywhere; for self-love is no more than the soothing of a man's self, which, done to another, is flattery. And though perhaps at this day it may be thought infamous, yet it is so only with them that are more taken with words than things.

Johann Amos Comenius (1592–1670) is often credited as the second great forefather of global education. A Catholic theologian like Erasmus, he opposed doctrinaire theology and supported the notion that nationality is subordinate to the universal knowledge that comes from God. Comenius was the first to suggest that schools had a role in promoting international understanding. His philosophical approach led to the coining of the term "pansophism," a method to reach a "peaceable kingdom." He purported that this kingdom could be realized if schools were turned into places where narrow doctrinal differences were cast aside and humane learning allowed to dominate. In 1957, the Member States of UNESCO paid homage to the great thinker Comenius on his 400th birthday by describing him as "one of the first men to propagate the ideas which UNESCO took for its guidance at the time of its establishment."

Security Concerns

Many educators have been slow to take up these new opportunities. There are a number of impediments we'll review. Andy Carvin is responsible for National Public Radio's web 2.0 outreach, and a pioneer in recognizing the social significance of the Internet. Carvin observed in the companion video to this book, many schools have had difficulty even accepting web 1.0. By rights, cautious educators believe that security concerns should limit Internet access. They have often heavily filtered their networks, resulting in student and teacher frustration as they try to search the web for content. In a web 2.0 world, with the increase in information and access, administrators have become even more anxious.

Chapter 1 • Global Education and the Web 2.0 Revolution

Andy Carvin, National Public Radio

With the birth of the Internet, suddenly borders became almost meaningless. You could as easily have some kind of conversation or collaboration with someone 5,000 miles away as you could with your neighbor.

We can no longer see the classroom as isolated by four walls or by borders. There is too much opportunity out there. Students all over the world—especially in parts of the Pacific Rim and Europe—have access to ubiquitous broadband on their mobile phones. These are the people who are going to create the next Googles and Microsofts and are going to be the next set of innovators.

Some countries have taken it upon themselves to see the Internet as an incubator for technological skills that children could use to help raise overall skills as well as advance overall economic opportunities. For example, there is a project that has been online for a very long time now called *ThinkQuest* in which students create educational websites as part of a global competition. If you go back ten years you could see a lot of really great projects from all over the world and a lot of competitive projects from the U.S., because when educators back then were using the Internet in the classroom, it was usually because no one was really aware of what they were doing, so you could get away with things and treat them as interesting experiments with their students.

Meanwhile, since then, our classrooms have been wired to the hilt, and there is Internet access all over the place, but when you look at the winners of these same projects—many of the winners tend to be students from Hong Kong, China, Germany, and it is because in many cases the school systems there have mobilized to embrace these contests as opportunities to achieve prestige on a global scale—to show that their students can be technologically innovative and innovative with content as well, and they see it in their interest, whereas in the U.S., you see who is winning these contests: it is often home-schooled kids, kids in private schools, kids in charter schools. You will still see kids in regular public schools [winning] as well,

> but they are not dominant in the way they used to be, even when Internet access wasn't ubiquitous.
>
> And so I think schools today and teachers today feel so many pressures from other forces, whether it's educational requirements to teach and prepare students for certain standardized tests; whether it's using certain Internet filtering to protect students from online safety concerns (but doing it in such a way that teachers don't have the ability to override those filters)—it kind of created a situation in which the Internet is being used as one big reference tool. If students need to know something, they look it up and go back to work, and it is not seen as a tool for innovation and collaboration and creativity. That concerns me. There is an opportunity that has been lost there.
>
> Andy Carvin (Quote from companion video, May 21, 2007)

The security and filtering concerns mentioned can be minimized through the use of smart policies. Teachers in Victoria, Australia, for example, are asked to require parental permission if students are going to be blogging or engaging online in some way. Further parameters might include blogging accounts created in the teacher's, rather than the student's, name. The student could be made an authorized participant in the blog. Teachers may also decide not to allow comments to be received on the blog (comments can instead be directed to an e-mail address that is provided). Another security measure is to make sure that permission to participate in the project is obtained from the building principal, the ultimate party responsible for any potential misconduct.

2

Pathways to Global Education

In this book, we'll examine pathways to global education, and we'll address critical implementation issues, such as support and mentoring, planning, and ways to overcome perceived or real barriers. I suggest you take your time and find your own path—for there is no quick and easy way to become a global educator.

Here are three possible pathways; they are not exclusive:

- Empathy for Others
- Finding New Ways to Enrich and Engage
- Desire for Social Justice

These suggestions represent conduits through which you and your students could begin or enrich existing global education strategies. The Empathy for Others pathway has its roots in what was formerly called International Education, which stressed the need to get to know the world through **cultural exchanges** and pen pal communications. The Finding New Ways to Enrich and Engage pathway reflects traditional social studies and the burgeoning interest in the concept of global citizenship, where loyalties to the planet, as well as our own countries, form a foundation for the understanding of critical issues, such as climate change, disease eradication, global terrorism, and the need for a broader global context and interdisciplinary approaches. The Desire for

Social Justice pathway represents the tradition of peace studies that sprang from world war conflicts in the early and middle parts of the 20th century.

Let's discuss each pathway by drawing on the experiences of several awarding-winning global educators.

Pathway: Empathy for Others

The essence of this pathway might begin with a moment in childhood when a youngster feels an instant of empathy with someone who has had to struggle, sometimes just for survival or to obtain a basic right. An example is explained by Sherry McAulliffe, a high school advanced placement (AP) history and American government teacher, as she remembers herself at the age of six:

> I was walking hand in hand with my grandma in a snow storm in Brooklyn so she could vote. I was about six years old. She talked about how important the process was, because in most of the world you do not have these opportunities to participate in government, especially the country she, nine sisters, and one brother left behind, Russia (circa early 1900s). It was through my grandma's eyes, gestures, and voice that I learned the importance of being part of a global community.

Later on, through her work in the women's and environmental movements and labor struggles, protesting along with César Chávez for the rights of migrant workers and assisting in the start of the very first Earth Day celebration, McAulliffe continued her commitment to global issues. Passing on her commitment to her children, she states,

> Both my sons know the meaning of actively participating to make the world better for others, that volunteering is an integral part of their lives. My oldest son, Adam, is actively serving in the Peace Corps in Ghana, since 2005. I instilled in my sons that we do not just talk about volunteering, we must do it and assist in eliminating poverty and hunger for all peoples around the globe.

McAulliffe continues to exhibit her passion for global education and justice and has won the U.S. State Department's Doors to Diplomacy competition.

That sense of empathy for others can be experienced through the eyes of a student in your own classroom. It might propel you, as it did award-winning teacher Ann

Lambert, to become a more globally aware teacher. When Lambert started offering ePal communications with her students during the 1990s, she noted:

> We only had one or two Internet-connected computers in the whole school. I saw immediate change in a sixth grade girl—a Title I free lunch and breakfast student who considered herself the poorest of the poor—who received an e-mail from a Korean girl describing her as rich. She could not believe that another person considered her rich. She soon began to complain less about her prospects, and she began to e-mail people all over the world during her lunch hour. She had found a new world and a new view of herself.

Pathway: Finding New Ways to Enrich and Engage

This pathway does not necessarily start as the first one did, from a simple human desire to meet and get to know our neighbors, but rather begins with a set of questions. These are big questions, such as: How do events in one part of the world affect the way we live in our home environments? What are other countries doing about the threat of climate change? What can we do to avoid a global pandemic? How can we lessen terrorist threats? Can we find a way to contain the global thirst for energy?

This pathway may spring from a teacher question. Marsha Goren, an Israeli English language learner (ELL) teacher and winner of many international awards, found herself "puzzled and apprehensive" when the first computers started arriving at her school. She began to think: "How am I going to cope with that little box and screen?" She tells an amusing anecdote of how she solicited a sixth grader to help her with her computer skills in exchange for English lessons after school. When the sessions began getting a bit tiring for both of them, she asked him if he were willing to give up the extra hours of English since he had improved so much. She said, "Maybe you don't need the English lessons anymore." He said, "I don't need the English lessons, but you still need the computer lessons. You have not yet received a 95!"

Goren realized that she was now on a journey: "I needed to advance my students and myself towards the world of tomorrow and not continue to educate them for a world that no longer existed." That journey then began when she joined an online program, Friends and Flags, and began to see how she could help her students learn English in fun and exciting ways by pairing them with students from other countries on a variety of creative projects.

CASE STUDY

Marsha Goren's Journey as a Globaldreamer

Marsha Goren, Personal Correspondence, April 29, 2007

Seven years ago I was looking for ways to interest my students in their English studies. After many courses and difficult work, I realized the value of the Internet as a way of spreading an educational message around the world. The process has led me to become a technology innovator and global leader in online collaborative learning projects. These projects now include thousands of children from more than 37 countries worldwide.

I knew I wanted to be a global educator after the incredible experience the students and I had when we participated in Friends and Flags, an online program here in Israel that reached out globally to bring students from different countries together. As an ELL teacher it was my wish to combine English teaching along with technology. I wanted my students to experience a social, cultural, and personal learning experience. The Friends and Flags project utilizes Internet technologies for genuine learning of the English language by activating and motivating students with various online activities. In addition to the utilization of technologies, studying English will also assist different cultures in participating with greater understanding in the challenge of globalization.

After I joined Friends and Flags, Globaldreamers was born. Its first named incarnation was "Dream a Dream with Ein Ganim" (my school). Globaldreamers is a nickname that stuck. Globaldreamers invites teachers throughout the world to share their "friendship projects"—projects where students post pictures, stories, or artwork around a theme that connects them to other students, such as helping improve the environment.

Globaldreamers has brought much pride and joy to Ein Ganim School; its principal, Hedy Rosenthal; the staff; and the students. The educational awards that Globaldreamers has received have come after long hard work and determination. Such awards include the Global SchoolNet Online Shared Learning award, the worldwide Microsoft Innovative Teachers award, the U.S. Global Collaboration award, and the prestigious Yad Vashem award for excellence in Holocaust teaching.

The dream is not over yet. We have only just begun.

Cheryl Vitali's experiences traveling as a young child and the memory of her teachers, who managed to enrich their classrooms through travel, helped turn Vitali's classrooms into places filled with travel posters. And, once she realized the power of technology to connect to the world in order to enrich and engage her students, there was no stopping her or her students.

CASE STUDY

Early Experiences on the Path to Becoming a Global Educator

Cheryl Vitali, Internet Educator of the Year 2000, Classroom Connect Personal Correspondence, June 15, 2007

My parents were responsible for the early experiences that intrigued me and led to my interest in global education. Ever since I was born, they traveled as much as they could, most of it car camping, and they took us all over the United States, parts of Canada, and Mexico. My father's aeronautical engineering work kept us moving quite a bit, and I attended six schools by fifth grade, ending up in San Jose, California. When I was in high school, my parents began bringing foreign exchange students into the home, as well as other visitors from several different countries; and they kept this up the remainder of their lives. I was extremely active in Girl Scouts and spent summers in camps, traveling with troops, and working out of state.

I can also attribute my interest to some of my teachers, especially Mr. Tindell in sixth grade, because he traveled extensively in South America for our social studies curriculum, and Mrs. Rutherford, who traveled through Europe for the humanities curriculum in high school. They both made learning memorable and along with some other outstanding teachers set the bar extremely high for what I desired to bring to my students. This was prior to current technologies, yet they were both global educators long before the advent of the Internet.

Thus far, I have 30 years' experience in education, working with all ranges of ages and abilities. My first classroom in 1977 was decorated with travel posters from other countries. I was teaching a self-contained seventh/eighth grade in a rural area and coaching sports as well. The position was temporary, yet my skill with diversifying instruction to a broad range of needs led to my entering into special education in 1978. I eventually became a resource specialist, teaching six or seven different grade levels on any given day. I enjoyed the breadth of curriculum and the challenge of meeting diverse needs. I was also always looking for ways to motivate my students and give them experiences that would broaden their horizons.

I had been rolling in a computer once a week and finally had a desktop with a local area network (LAN) that I immediately began using with students in the spring of 1993. When I heard about telecommunications in 1993, I was immediately hooked, even before I really understood what it was. I always wanted to be a pioneer and applied to be part of the **California Telemation Project** as a telementor. In the process, I established the first Internet connection in our district, stretched our LAN to ridiculous levels, developed the first website for our community, and became involved in developing, designing, and contributing to a variety of global communities. In the later 1990s, I started a group called the Musketeers with Joan Goble and Rene de Vries, among others. These world-class global educators, along with several others, have continued to do incredible things with their students.

I did these projects with my students and with students in an after-school Tech Club in the upper grades. Our equipment has never been the most cutting edge, yet the student's enthusiasm has always been great. I saw values with this in helping children perceive the world and themselves in ways that were never possible when just using more traditional methodologies.

Pathway: Desire for Social Justice

Many who desire a personal experience of serving others choose this path. This pathway often leads to the development of skills necessary for conflict resolution and for helping people, no matter what their ethnic, religious, or cultural backgrounds, to live in harmony. Karrie Dietz, a teacher at a Catholic high school, related to me how she developed a sense of social justice while attending the College of St. Catherine in St. Paul, Minnesota, where community action was emphasized. She told me, "Teachers at each grade level were encouraged to develop and engage students in three community service projects each year. I recognized the benefits of connecting students with their local community." It's not every teacher who shares Dietz's taste for adventure—she and her husband moved to Tashkent, Uzbekistan, in 2000. But the need to find challenging materials for her students, who came from 40 countries, made her a firm believer in global education.

> "If all students were able to do collaborative projects, they would have a much better understanding of global issues."
>
> *Eliane Metni, Syrian iEARN co-coordinator*

Chris Plutte, featured on the companion video and co-founder of Global Nomads Group, wanted to find some way to replicate the experience of a voyage at sea that he took when he was in high school. During the voyage, students from all over the world discovered shared interests and forged powerful friendships. He found a way to study at an international university in Paris. And, with three of his friends, he founded Global Nomads as a way to enable more students to share the type of rich global awareness and friendships he experienced.

From the Global Nomads Group website (www.gng.org):

> Established in 1998, the Global Nomads Group (GNG) is an international NGO that creates interactive educational programs for students about global issues. GNG's educational programs include (1) four types of videoconferences—The PULSE, Currents, Innovations, and Rapid Response—where students learn about and discuss subjects with their peers from around the world in live, facilitated sessions; and (2) videos and learning content on a variety of international issues relevant to teachers and students.

All GNG programs are directly linked to school curricula, education standards and 21st-century learning objectives and are accompanied by lesson plans and training for teachers. Programs are broadcast during the school day and cover a range of topics in the curriculum, including civics, social and global studies, geography, world history, science, economics, and politics.

In its 10-year history, the Global Nomads Group has conducted programs in more than 40 countries and reached more than 1 million young people. Each year, as many as 10,000 students participate in GNG's interactive programs, which have been recognized for their educational value and innovation with awards from the Goldman Sachs Foundation and United States Distance Learning Association.

HISTORICAL INTERLUDE

Opposing Viewpoints: John Dewey and Ellwood P. Cubberley

Only after the experience of two world wars, with their savage waste of human life, was there a large opening for progressive thinkers to rethink the role nationalism played in American schools.

One such progressive thinker whose influence grew throughout the early 20th century was John Dewey. He had witnessed an extraordinary influx of immigrants into his home city of Chicago.

> It is said that one ward in the city of Chicago has forty different languages represented in it. It is a well-known fact that some of the largest Irish, German, and Bohemian cities in the world are located in America, not in their own countries.... No educational system can be regarded as complete until it adopts into itself the various ways in which social and intellectual intercourse may be promoted, and employs them systematically ... to make them positive causes in raising the whole level of life.

Dewey held a great devotion to democracy and viewed it as an active ingredient of educational experiences. To practice democratic thinking meant to interact continuously with those from different cultures and backgrounds as a way to enrich one's own understanding of the world. Remembered as a great educator,

Dewey argued vigorously against the encroachment of military values in schools at a time of great patriotic fervor during the First World War—viewing such efforts as the opposite of education, in that they sought to indoctrinate children. He is quoted as saying, "As a society becomes more enlightened, it realizes that it is responsible not to transmit and conserve the whole of its existing achievements, but only such as make for a better future society. The school is the chief agency for the accomplishment of this end."

The great proponent of a contrary view to Dewey's was the historian and administrator Ellwood P. Cubberley, who held the view that the new immigrants who came to American shores in the 19th century had "little to offer" the new country from their own cultures, traditions, and customs.

Cubberley saw his mission as remaking them as Americans and separating them from their former ethnic identities. Cubberley's negative view of immigrants is betrayed by his clinical language as he referred to "these people" who "settle in groups or settlements, and set up their national manners, customs, and observances." He believed that "our task" was "to break up these groups of people as part of our American race, and to implant in their children, so far as it can be done, the Anglo-Saxon conception of righteousness" (Cubberley, 1909, pp. 15–16).

Most 21st-century teachers interested in global teaching and learning would agree with Dewey's philosophy that advocates learning from those in different cultures, rather than Cubberley's mission to separate immigrants from their original languages and cultures. ELL teachers play a particularly sensitive role as they teach new American students English while showing respect for and interest in their languages and cultures of origin.

Support and Mentoring

No matter how you find your pathway, creating a global classroom is not easy. Even the global pioneers interviewed for this book needed to be supported in their efforts by a community and often by an individual facilitator. Many teachers attend workshops and then find their way to online communities that support them in their quest. Joan Goble, whom you will meet in the following case study, has been particularly fortunate at finding partners online. She writes about how one thing led to another after an initial workshop whetted her appetite. One such online community, Web 66, (predating Global Schoolhouse) led her to a project hosted by an Australian school. She began by e-mailing the coordinator to ask how her students could get involved:

> I told her I was a newbie, and she took me under her wing, so to speak. She helped my students and me so much! Our involvement in this project helped me to realize the great power of using the Internet as a tool for research and collaboration.

Following that project Goble was also connected with a teacher with whom she clicked right away:

> I began collaborating with another teacher in this project, Rene de Vries, from the Netherlands. Since then, we have not only had our students working together on many different projects, from Travel Buddies exchanges to progressive stories and more, but we have over the past nine years co-hosted four successful, award-winning international collaborative projects, which included many other schools from literally all over the world!

The message that comes through quite clearly from Goble's experiences is that part of becoming a global teacher is being venturesome enough to go online and collaborate with others. Her path led from finding a compatible online collaborator, to experiencing success with that collaboration, to wanting to do more and more because the enthusiasm and motivation level of the students was now piqued as a result of this great start.

Another example of the value of collaboration and mentoring comes from Karrie Dietz, who teaches at Tashkent International School in Uzbekistan and talks about her first project with a school in Termez, Uzbekistan, in 2003:

> We did forums, work exchanges, and finally a teacher exchange visit with that school. Even today we look on our first Uzbek partners as the ones most likely to be faithful to extended projects. Their collaboration really opened the eyes of our students to a part of the world they did not know well.

These partnerships sustain teachers, particularly those who feel beleaguered when they don't receive encouragement and support from their colleagues.

CASE STUDY

The Power of Mentoring and Collaboration

Joan Goble, Personal Correspondence, April 30, 2007

Joan Goble has always been an innovator. She was one of the first to pilot what became known in Indiana as the Buddy Project in 1988. For this project, families with children in fourth through sixth grades received home computers, and teachers received professional development to support curriculum goals. Goble was fortunate to find mentors and collaborators who took her early interest in technology to new levels.

> I kept on keeping on with what technology our school had, and every chance I got, I went to workshops about computer use in the classroom. In the summer of 1995, I went to a workshop that showed us how to get online using a dial-up connection. That was when I knew I wanted to get online in my classroom!
>
> It was in the fall of 1996, when my school obtained a 56K line to the Internet, that I was lucky enough to win a grant to obtain an Internet-ready computer. I had been to a workshop that summer that demonstrated many ways to get students involved in online projects. That workshop hooked me on using the Internet in my own classroom! I had heard of Web 66, so I searched there to find a school, preferably from another country, that had online projects for other schools to join. (I had not heard of Global Schoolhouse at that time.)
>
> I saw many interesting projects, but it was the Trees and Forests Project, hosted by Elanora Heights Primary School of Sydney, Australia, that caught my attention the most. I decided to e-mail the coordinator, Judith Bennett, to ask how my students could get involved. I told her I was a newbie, and she took me under her wing, so to speak. She helped my students and me so much!
>
> Our involvement in this project helped me to realize the great power of using the Internet as a tool for research and collaboration. The Internet is the best motivator I have ever seen! The whole experience of the Trees and Forest Project was wonderful; however, one special thing happened that changed my teaching forever. I began collaborating with another teacher in this project, Rene de Vries, from the Netherlands. Since then, we have not only had our students working together on many different projects from Travel Buddy exchanges to progressive stories and more, but we have over the past nine years co-hosted four successful, award-winning international collaborative projects which include many other schools from literally all over the world! I am very happy about the successes we

have had with these online projects, and I love to share the stories of these with other educators, because I truly believe in the Internet as a wonderful teaching tool!

Our Collaborations

After the Trees and Forests project ended, Rene and I decided to create our own collaborative project and to invite schools from all over the world to join in. So, over the summer of 1997 we worked (online of course, since we were on two different continents) on TENAN: The Endangered Animals of the World (www.tenan.vuurwerk.nl). This project invites students from all over the world to research and report on animals from their area or around the world that are endangered or threatened, and we publish their findings on this site.

TENAN was launched with the help of Global SchoolNet's project registry in the fall of 1997 and has been online and active ever since. At this point, after nine years, we have had more than 100 schools enter over 1,500 reports. Our project did so well the first few months that it won an award from Childnet International! This allowed Rene and me to meet in person, when we and other winners were flown to London to receive our award. It was wonderful finally to meet Rene, after having collaborated with him online for nearly a year. We have been friends ever since.

We kept TENAN going, and decided to create more projects: TESAN: The Endangered Species and Nature of the World.

Launched in the fall of 1998, www.tesan.vuurwerk.nl invites students from all over the world to better understand the numbers of endangered species through sharing and collaboration.

Animal Diaries:

Launched in the fall of 1999, www.tesan.vuurwerk.nl/diaries invites children from around the world to research the world of animals from the animal's point of view, as if they were composing a journal.

City Quest:

Launched in the fall of 2001, www.cityquest.nl provides a model way to organize a collaboration among students in two or three schools who research the historical importance of their own cities and share their information in graphic and text form, so that all participating students can compare and contrast the cities.

These projects were very active for many years, but in recent years they have seen a decline in schools and classrooms joining and actually following through. This could be for many reasons. One of them is teachers, at least in the United States, are finding it harder and harder to have time to devote to any online collaborations when we find ourselves spending most of our time testing or preparing students to take tests.

Rene and I discussed this recently and have decided to maybe end the projects as far as their active status in the next year, but we'll keep the content online (all free—through Vuurwerk in the Netherlands) because we feel they are very beneficial for our students as well as others. If we see more teachers interested in them, then we will start them back up again.

These projects opened doors for Rene and me and, of course, our students! As I mentioned, TENAN won a Childnet award, which allowed us to finally meet in person.

In 1998 Rene and I were asked to join a group called GET (Global Educators Team): www.get.vuurwerk.nl/.

This organization gave us the opportunity to interact and collaborate with other like-minded educators. One wonderful meeting our GET team had was in China, when we met to help dedicate a new wing to the Tianjin University in Tianjin, China, in the fall of 2002. We were all made to feel so very welcome there! One highlight of that trip was getting to walk on the Great Wall. At about the same time, Rene introduced me to another group of teachers, not officially organized but very active in online e-mail discussions. Cheryl Vitali was the leader, and we all ended up calling our little group The Musketeers. Both of these groups have given me support and encouragement, mostly because we believe in the power of online collaborations.

One more great opportunity that came my way, mostly due to reading all of my e-mails, was the chance to apply to visit Japan in the Fulbright Memorial Fund Teacher Program. I was able to do this in the summer of 2003. I met many great teachers there, some from the States, and many, many from Japan. I would tell you all about this, but it is better if you visit my website: www.siec.k12.in.us/cannelton/fmfjapan/.

Collaboration and Lesson Planning

As you've read, it makes a difference to your lesson planning when you're working with a partner you can trust. Some of the work of exact planning is taken off your shoulders when you have a shared understanding with your partner of how to sustain the course or module you are teaching.

Karrie Dietz speaks about meeting a Kentucky teacher online in connection with a Friendship through Education project after 9/11. She says, "We know what to expect from each other regarding frequency and content of student correspondence. We try new projects, but we are both patient and understanding when they do not work as anticipated (i.e., PowerPoint doesn't open)." The trust factor is built up slowly—in Joan Goble's case, it took a year for her to feel comfortable and in synch with her partner from the Netherlands. The beginning experience helps to build confidence that the global connections not only work, but produce real educational value. From that first piloting, the result is often that the teachers and the students want to involve more classes in global collaborations.

Karrie Dietz recommends this next sequence of planning activities:

Stage 1: I begin by collaborating with colleagues (other teachers and specialists) to discuss what we want students to know, understand, and be able to do as an outcome.

Stage 2: Next, we decide how the learning will be evidenced (assessments). We aim for contextual assessments, those that are meaningful and authentic.

Stage 3: Finally, we identify what experiences (learning activities) can prepare students for the assessments.

During the planning process, keep collaboration in mind: whom in the school, local, and global community can our students collaborate with?

HISTORICAL INTERLUDE

Mid- to Late Twentieth Century

Following the shock and dreadfulness of the Second World War, Americans became more interested in the rest of the world. A culture and society began to emerge where isolationism could no longer thrive. The establishment of organizations such as the United Nations and the World Bank signaled a new era of multinational cooperation and dialogue.

The term "global education" was coined in 1969 by Pulitzer Prize recipient René Dubos. During the following decades, use of this term, along with terms like "international education," "world studies," and "peace education," became more widespread.

Global Education and the Development of 21st-Century Skills

During the 1980s and 1990s, a number of developments raised the visibility of global education in the United States. Reports emerged declaring that American students were failing to keep pace with their international peers in science and math. The media widely reported that U.S. students were outperformed by the Pacific Rim nations. In 1985, the Council of Chief State School Officers issued a policy statement on international dimensions in education that would have wide influence. U.S. students needed improved language skills and increased knowledge of math and science. The term "21st-century skills" was soon on the lips of educational decision makers, government officials, and industry leaders. These skills included learning about other cultures as an

> integrated part of their study of literature, history, social studies, natural sciences, the arts, and other courses throughout the curriculum. Only by learning about other cultures, faiths, and ways of living will [students] be able to better their understanding of the various perspectives that frame our world and the people who inhabit it (Council of Chief State School Officers, 2006).

A coalition of business groups and education leaders formed the Partnership for 21st-Century Skills to advocate on state and national levels for the infusion of 21st-century skills into the curriculum. Tools and resources had to be provided to help support changes that included global awareness, civic and business literacy, collaborative skills, and problem-solving skills. As part of this tide, information technology and media literacy skills were also tagged as critical.

The resurgence of global issues in the 21st century has much to do with the recognition that in the wake of accelerating globalization, the nation state is no longer the all-powerful entity it once was. Heads of global corporations are joining with national leaders to remind schools that we now live in an interdependent world. Educators are rethinking the curriculum, and technology is changing the way we teach and learn. Today's educators must work with students to understand what it is like to live in a multicultural society and to develop a sense of global citizenship.

Accountability Pressures

The most common resistance to getting started with global education is the fear of detracting from the need to teach to state standards and assessments. These kind of accountability pressures are so real in many schools today that even subjects like physical education, music, and art have been significantly reduced in length of class time or have been removed completely from the curriculum.

Taking a closer look at what today's subject area standards are requiring of teachers, it is clear that teaching a globally-aware curriculum is not a diversion, but an essential part of fostering a 21st-century learning environment. For example, even when it comes to algebra, there can be a global dimension. The Virginia algebra standards require students to "represent, model, analyze, or solve mathematical or real world problems." Math Process Standard (7.0D1) requires students to "relate or apply mathematics within the discipline to other disciplines and to life." The fourth goal of Missouri's global standards calls for students to "analyze the duties and responsibilities of individuals in societies."

Missouri's civics standards for Grades 5–8 ask, "What is the relationship of the United States to other nations and to world affairs?" And further: "How is the world organized politically? How has the United States influenced other nations and how have other nations influenced American politics and society?"

The U.S. National Science Education Standards have a section for Grades 5–8 concerning the place of science in society, including understanding how science and technology "have advanced through contributions of many different people, in different cultures, at different times in history." Further, students are required to understand how science and technology have "contributed enormously to economic growth and productivity among societies and groups within societies." Teachers are asked to help students understand various global threats to the world's ecosystem.

All these standards present direct opportunities to inject a global perspective. (See Appendix C for a complete list of the National Educational Technology Standards for Students, Teachers, and Administrators, and how they connect to global issues.) For example, students are to "develop cultural understanding and global awareness by engaging with learners of other cultures, [and] contribute to project teams to produce original works or solve problems."

Some of the best educational minds have perceived a need for all students to become more globally aware, to see their humanity reflected in people living in lands and cultures remote from their own, and to appreciate cultural differences as opportunities to learn and to grow. Many pathways lead to toward global learning; whichever you choose, rest assured your journey will deepen your teaching and increase your students' level of engagement and passion for learning.

3

The Flat Classroom Project

One example of the new web 2.0 collaborative culture is the wiki, "a freely expandable collection of interlinked webpages; a hypertext system for storing and modifying information; a database, where each page is easily edited by any user with a forms-capable web browser client" (Schwartz, Clark, Cossarin, & Rudolph, 2004). Wikis provide students with a wonderful collaborative space where they can build and refine their knowledge through the use of digital editing and revision tools.

What Is the Flat Classroom Project?

We've learned a great deal about the application of wikis to global learning in recent years through the groundbreaking work of two teachers in particular—one located first in Bangladesh, then in Qatar, and now in Beijing, China (Julie Lindsay), and one located in Georgia, in the U.S. (Vicki Davis). These two have taken it upon themselves to create award-winning linkages between the schools in their countries. Their Flat Classroom Project explored Tom Friedman's best-selling book, *The World Is Flat* (2007). The goal was to find out how today's turbo-charged information age contributes to the major social and economic changes occurring across the globe.

For the first Flat Classroom Project in 2006, 23 students in two classrooms were grouped in pairs to explore topics presented in Friedman's book by using a variety of communication and multimedia web 2.0 tools including wikis, Skype, YouTube, Flickr, Blogger, and Evoca.

This pioneering project illustrated the wiki's educational value for global educators. Davis, one co-designer of the project, explained in an interview published on her blog why she used wikis: "I felt that wikis would work well in a collaborative/cooperative environment because of how well they mark and denote the exact contributions of students. A wiki also documents very well the discussions that take place between students to arrive at a certain place of knowledge and their agreement on fact" (Davis, 2008).

In the first Flat Classroom Project, students were subdivided in groups of two with one student from Dhaka, Bangladesh, and one student from the United States. They explored a "flattening trend" (the various Internet-inspired developments that promote faster ways to harness and communicate knowledge). Some of the criteria for evaluating effectiveness of the resulting wiki content included the use of hyperlinks in the text "to show you are an expert on the topic," and the use of sound and video to "effectively enhance the message and provide another element of understanding and interest." Students were also evaluated on their use of RSS feeds, automated electronic searches for relevant news and information. Students posted information about their work periodically via a blog. They produced videos and were given credit for clear and meaningful content and quality of video editing.

Blogging's Role

Flat Classroom teachers treat student blogs much like logs that can help them track student progress and assist in classroom communication. The blog also provides a way for everyone to feel connected to the classroom and exchange information. The material can be archived and reviewed anytime and anywhere. The project also incorporates collaborative wiki reports and **digital stories**, including explicit guidelines in how to **storyboard** the project.

Following are examples of how wikis are used in Flat Classroom projects. For starters, there's a map students can use to locate themselves. Additional wiki resources include project calendars, topic listings, and rubrics available for both teachers and students.

Students can communicate via podcasts, postings on blogs, and by answering questions posted on the wikis. They can communicate in real time via videoconferencing or asynchronously using video clips. In the Flat Classroom Project, the collaborating teachers gave instructions to student pairs using blogs as a communication tool.

Podcasts and Vodcasts

Flat Classroom Project students often begin by learning how to use podcasts. They start with a relatively simple podcasting tool such as Evoca, an easy tool that helps to prepare voice recordings so students can introduce themselves to each other.

The students use podcasting technology along with video (vodcast) to "effectively enhance the message and provide another element of understanding and interest" using **Windows Movie Maker**. See: http://flatclassroomproject2006.wikispaces.com/Rubrics/.

Podcasts were also used to enable the international team of judges to discuss and share their final evaluations of the students' portfolio of work. The discussion podcast is entitled Judging the Flat Classroom Project.

Skype and Similar Tools

Skype (www.skype.com) uses **Voice over Internet Protocol (VoIP)** to allow not just audio, but also videoconferencing, **file sharing**, and **instant messaging**, among up to ten people, connected to two computers that have the Skype software installed. (When used in a group conferencing format, the term **skypecast** is used). Both the software and the use of the communication tool is free. Students are expected to be in regular contact with their wiki partner. Skype was used for the Flat Classroom Project but because it is often blocked by school security a similar tool is now used, Elluminate (www.elluminate.com).

The teachers provide several lessons regarding security issues involved with videoconferencing, such as don't reveal your full personal information. They also provide students with practice using the system by calling each other and the teacher and using the messaging functions that allow them to comment on a call (even though their microphone is muted through the instant messaging facility). Only when the teacher is fully satisfied that no abuse can take place will he or she allow videoconferencing to be used for its twin functions—to host expert speakers and to help maintain regular interactions with fellow students thousands of miles away.

See Julie Lindsay's step-by-step account about using VoIP in the classroom: http://julielindsay.wikispaces.com/VoIP/.

Classroom Ning

Ning (www.ning.com) is a social networking tool that functions much like a wiki—with interlinked webpages that create room for dialogue among all those with an account. Unlike a wiki, the Ning tool can be used to create public or personal pages that can be decorated according to students' personal tastes (students can choose from a range of templates, themes, and images) and to display students' favorite videos, podcasts, **widgets**, and so forth.

In the later stages of the Flat Classroom Project, the Ning functioned similarly to the way the blog worked. Ning provides educational social networking without ads—avoiding the potential exposure to suggestive ads that typically run in other social networking sites. Students post their "weekly reflections" and answers to the "ethical question of the week" in a private place where they have a lively open debate and share photos, videos, and podcasts.

Flat Classroom teachers are excited about positive student reactions to the Ning. It gets the communication out of private student e-mail accounts, where it cannot be properly supervised, and onto the Ning, which is connected to their e-mail anyway. This environment cannot be duplicated in any other manner that is as customizable, and even at school students like to customize their own pages.

The Flat Classroom and its successor project involving five classrooms highlighted the following principles and project strategies:

- Aligning project purpose, learning objective, content, and the NETS with product outcome

- **Scaffolding** to support students in their collaborative work through the use of relevant tools and online resources

- Preparing students with a knowledge of instructional design

Aligning Project Purpose, Learning Objective, Content, and the NETS with Product Outcome

The choice of assignments and decisions on how those assignments will be measured based on a rubric are of key importance. The Flat Classroom Project asks students to think critically about a variety of social and economic trends spurred by technology and to examine the impact of these trends on the students' lives as they prepare for the future. Each assignment is covered by the following criteria:

- Design and Technical Quality
- Synthesis and Construction of Ideas
- Online Engagement and Interaction with the Project
- Reflection and Evaluation

Figures 3.1–3.6 courtesy Flat Classroom Project by Julie Lindsay (http://123elearning.blogspot.com) and Victoria A. Davis (http://coolcatteacher.blogspot.com) at http://flatclassroomproject.org/.

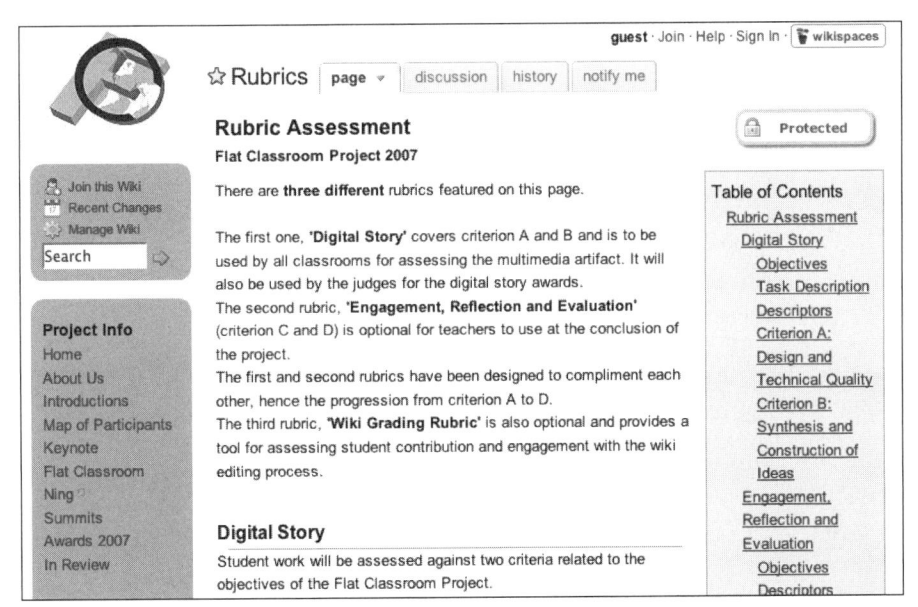

FIGURE 3.1 A screenshot from the Flat Classroom Project with details on using rubric assessments (Davis & Lindsay, 2007).

There is significant flexibility to adjust the assignment rubric to the learning objective—what is needed is clarity. So, for example, if we were to substitute having students look at how energy policy will change over the next ten years, and we wanted to connect this to a science project, we might review the standards for a high school science project. Helpful resources, rubrics, updates and the most accurate information can be accessed at http://flatclassroomproject.org/.

> **The National Educational Technology Standards for Students Standard for Communication and Collaboration**
>
> The National Educational Technology Standards (NETS) for both Teachers and Students have become a valuable tool for keeping up with identifying what students should know and be able to do to learn effectively using technology. The second edition of the Standards and Performance Indicators for Students includes under "Communication and Collaboration" the need [under 2 (c)] for students to communicate and collaborate at a distance to "develop cultural understanding and global awareness by engaging learners of other cultures." (NETS•S, 2007)
>
>> Students use digital media and communication environments to work collaboratively to support individual learning and contribute to the learning of others. Collaborations include:
>>
>> - Interact and co-publish with peers, experts, or others, employing a variety of digital environments and media
>> - Communicate information and ideas effectively to multiple audiences, using a variety of media and formats
>> - Develop cultural understanding and global awareness by engaging with learners of other cultures
>> - Contribute to project teams to produce original works or solve problems

Following are screenshots of the Flat Classroom portal and some of its many related networks and projects.

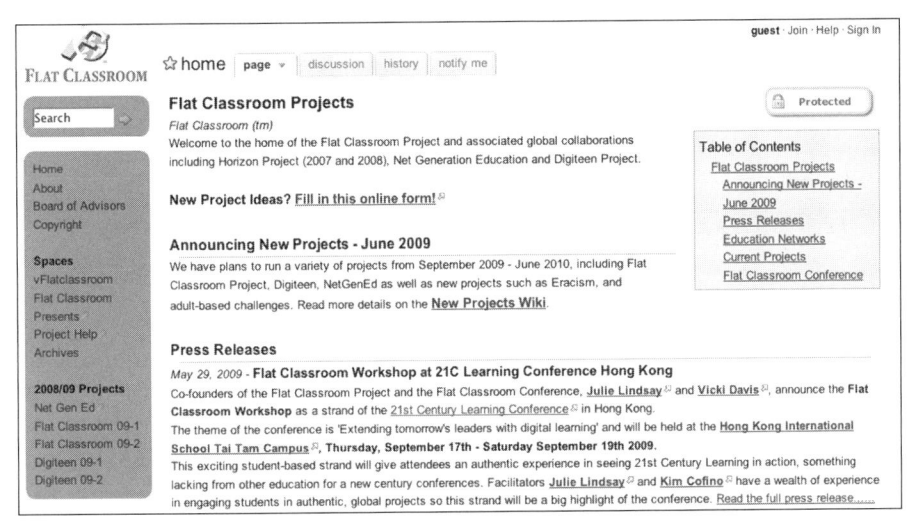

FIGURE 3.2 The Flat Classroom portal at http://flatclassroomproject.org

The Flat Classroom portal wiki (Figure 3.2) links to all projects and activities having to do with Flat Classroom. It includes announcements and press releases about new projects, international workshops, and other opportunities. It also includes links to all archived or past projects, workshops, and conference material.

Chapter 3 • The Flat Classroom Project

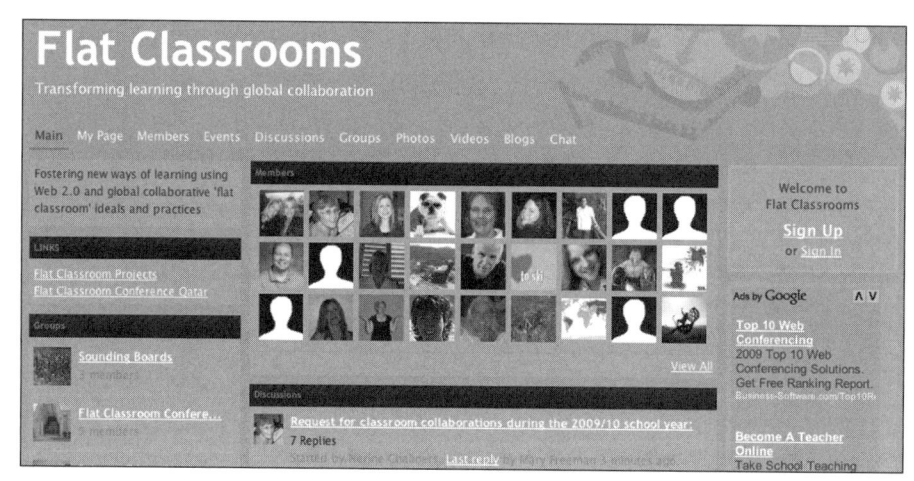

FIGURE 3.3 The Flat Classrooms educational network at http://flatclassrooms.ning.com

The purpose of the Flat Classrooms educational network (Figure 3.3) is to develop a learning community for educators globally and to support Flat Classroom workshops. Here, like-minded teachers, administrators, and supporters can find each other, propose new projects, and discuss global collaborations. This Ning does not allow student members; therefore, educators are at liberty to discuss and interact with a view towards planning and improving their pedagogy for Flat Classroom adventures.

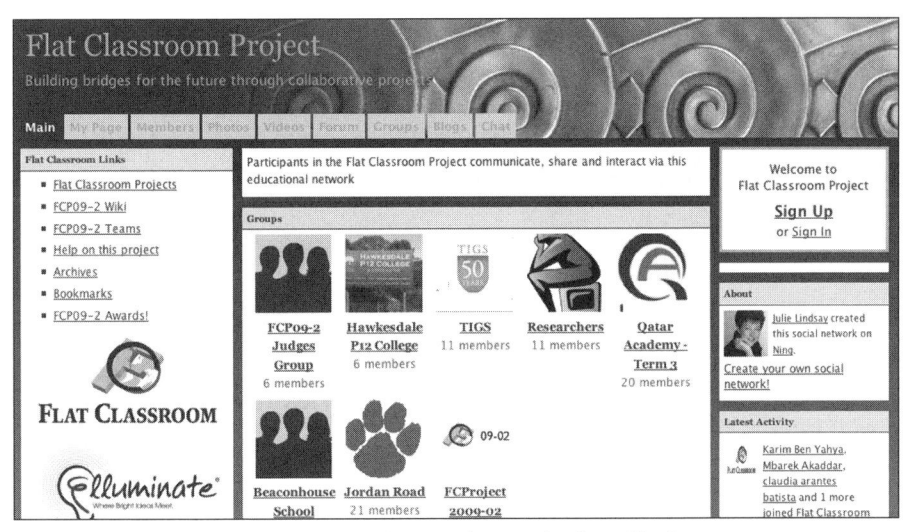

FIGURE 3.4 The Flat Classroom Project educational network at http://flatclassroomproject.ning.com

The Flat Classroom Project educational network (Figure 3.4) is for all past and present members and supporters of the Flat Classroom Project. This project now runs three times during the year and attracts a wide variety of international participants. Both educators and students are members of this Ning. Students in the project use this environment to blog, interact with their project partners, and post multimedia as part of the project requirements.

Chapter 3 • The Flat Classroom Project

FIGURE 3.5 The Digiteen Project educational network at http://digiteen.ning.com

This network was developed specifically for the Digiteen Project (Figure 3.5), a digital citizenship project for teenagers. Educators, supporters, and students can be members. Digiteen runs 3 times per year and also attracts a global set of participants. Students in the project use this Ning to interact with other students and teachers, blog, and post multimedia as needed.

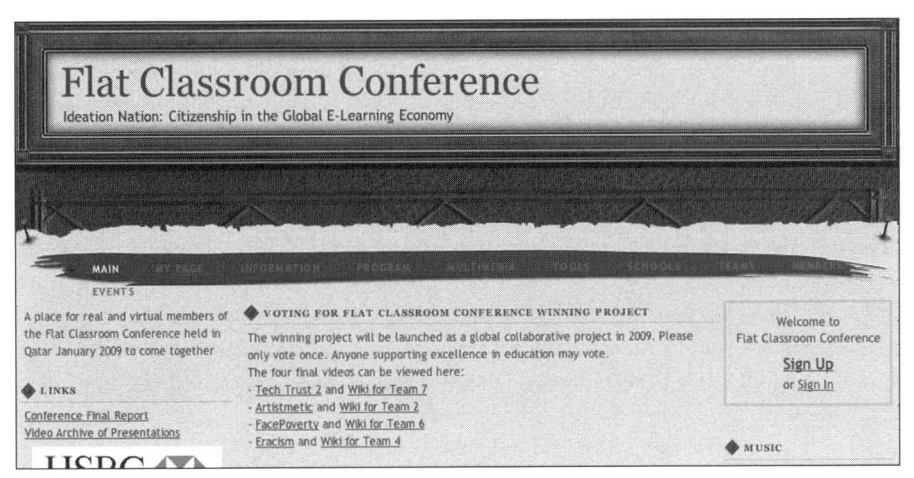

FIGURE 3.6 The Flat Classroom Conference educational network at http://flatclassroomconference.ning.com

The Flat Classroom Conference educational network Ning (Figure 3.6) was set up for the Flat Classroom Conference, held in Qatar in January, 2009. The conference attracted students and educators from all over the world. The Ning is an ongoing learning community designed to facilitate and promote further real-time Flat Classroom gatherings.

Preparing Students to Launch a Global Classroom

Julie Lindsay remarked in a blog post, "the thing that could most divide us in the future is cultural ignorance, which could erect virtual walls amidst the bits and bytes of Internet-based communications. We can be no more connected than the willingness of those who are connecting." (Lindsay, 2007)

Davis insists that students be prepared to connect with their peers and the world by understanding both the technical and the social demands of working with web 2.0 tools. She prepares her students first by giving them practice in using a number of the communication tools within the comfort and safety of their own classroom with their own classmates. She recommends first setting up a classroom Ning and a wiki, so students can practice creating appropriate messages. At this stage, you can also introduce tools such as Skype that can be used to create audiovisual conversations as well as instant messaging.

Next, connect all your students to the same Ning, giving them an opportunity to practice collaborating—sharing photos, videos, blogs, and so on. Running classrooms in this way helps the students to be socialized in the new mode of communication, and helps you to learn about potentially troublesome conduct and how to take appropriate action.

The next step: Have the students connect via Skype to another person or group. This is an essential step to model appropriate behavior and techniques. Following this, other aspects can be added, such as inviting a guest speaker to your classroom via Skype or another method of videoconferencing. Building a sense of a global audience is accomplished through students being granted permission from their parents to launch a public blog (or a large common blog such as **Youth Voices**); there students may interact with others around a topic they are interested in.

The final step is to work globally on a collaborative project: students exchange information necessary to produce a video or some other narrative product, using a Ning and a wiki to communicate.

Students can be exposed to what the Flat Classroom teachers refer to as a "keynote" or "thought leader" lecture from an expert.

Reviews of the Flat Classroom Project and others like it reveal how challenging a collaborative assignment can be. A transition from the Flat Classroom Project (with two classrooms connected) to the Horizon Project (with ten classrooms interconnected) was accomplished through an innovative idea: student management of the groups, with project and assistant managers and editors elected for each wiki, and the two teachers acting as facilitators to the other teachers to help make the entire project flow appropriately.

The Flat Classroom Project Inspires Others

Inspired in part by the example of the Flat Classroom Project, a number of teachers have begun to use wikis to enhance global collaboration. Two of the more notable projects are Mathlincs and 1001 Flat World Tales.

Mathlincs

Mathlincs is a collaborative project for fifth- and sixth-grade math students from around the world. The objectives of these collaborations are the following:

- Students learn to collaborate, communicate, and create with students in other places

- Students are engaged in real world math activities
- Students gain understanding by sharing their thoughts and ideas
- Teachers build partnerships with other teachers

The Mathlincs Project follows the same individualistic spirit driving the Flat Classroom project.

1001 Flat World Tales

Created by a teacher at the Korea International School, 1001 Flat World Tales (http://es1001tales2009.wikispaces.com) demonstrates how curriculum goals can be seamlessly integrated with global awareness to produce a fun and creative challenge for students that is motivating and exciting. Begun as a collaboration among three schools, the Korea International School (KIS) in Seoul, South Korea; Punahou High School in Honolulu, Hawaii; and Arapahoe High School in Littleton, Colorado; students engage in a writing prompt that is loosely taken from *Tales from 1001 Arabian Nights*—in which Scheherazade tells stories to please a sultan who threatens her life.

Students revise their own tales using six criteria (ideas, organization, and four others)—one each week—and use podcast technology to read their tales to each other. Thirty students collaborate to produce a book of their tales using Skype and podcasting. The teachers provide instructions using a video (screen cast) on how to use the wiki technologies: www.screencast-o-matic.com/watch/cijnoqvu/.

Simulations

The research firm Gartner recently released a study in which it estimated 80% of all active Internet users will have a virtual "second life" by the end of 2011 (Gartner, 2007). One website, Second Life (http://secondlife.com), has transformed the entire field of simulation, providing ease of access to **virtual reality** and enabling anyone to create characters and scenarios and interactions that take place in real time. Corporations and educational organizations have built three-dimensional-looking buildings in

> Global Kids' Digital Media Initiative recognizes in its mission statement that, "Since September 2001, the American people and our leaders have come to realize that a lack of knowledge about other countries and global issues seriously impedes our capacity to assure a secure and sustainable future."

Second Life that they use to promote their products or to provide educational experiences.

Second Life is exciting, but minors are not allowed—there are some X-rated features on the site. Instead, young people are directed to Teen Second Life (http://teen.secondlife.com). In 2006, Global Kids became the first organization to conduct public programs within the virtual world of Teen Second Life. They offer "experiential workshops," covering such topics as the genocide in Darfur, racism, and the digital divide, in collaboration with organizations like UNICEF, the United States Holocaust Memorial Museum, Youth Ventures, and others.

One of their projects asks students to role-play a poor family in Haiti (www.tigweb.org/tiged/projects/ayiti/game.html). They ask the question: "What is it like to live in poverty, struggling every day to stay healthy, keep out of debt, and get educated?" (Figure 3.7).

One teacher, after playing the game, made the following comment:

> The game, which is made in cooperation with UNICEF, drives home some pertinent, if sad, facts. The poor can achieve very moderate success in life and may be reduced to living in pitiful conditions if they should make the slightest mistake or encounter the slightest unforeseen hardship....The wonders of education, children needing to be children, not wage-earners—these are, in fact, luxuries our economic state allows us....Beautiful principles, indeed, but … how realistic?
>
> *(Global Kids' Digital Media Initiative, 2004)*

FIGURE 3.7 Global Kids offers high school students a game in which players take responsibility for a family of five in rural Haiti.

In another initiative, teenagers from around the world created a site on Teen Second Life to make students aware of sex trafficking. Reports on this initiative are found on the Global Kids blog (www.globalkids.org/?id=48). Another activity on Teen Second Life, Race to the Bottom, evoked the following response from one of the students in the virtual classroom:

> Basically, we were assigned a team of three and a third-world country to represent. And then we had to decide how much financial, legal, ethical, and other kinds of incentives we were going to give to a large corporation that was considering moving its labor to a foreign country to increase profits. The amazing part for me was when I realized that the name of the "game" wasn't random; it was directly related to what we were doing. So I tried to get everyone to take a stand against the corporation, and it didn't work. And I realized that's the problem we face today.
>
> *(Global Kids' Digital Media Initiative, 2007)*

4

iEARN

Although not quite the oldest, iEARN (International Education and Resource Network) is the largest school network. It features a more expansive international and professional development mission than any other network. It focuses more than any other network on the pedagogies involved in creating collaborative, project-based work and owes more than a debt of gratitude to the work of Freinet, but also to that of Dewey and Kilpatrick.

Chapter 4 • iEARN

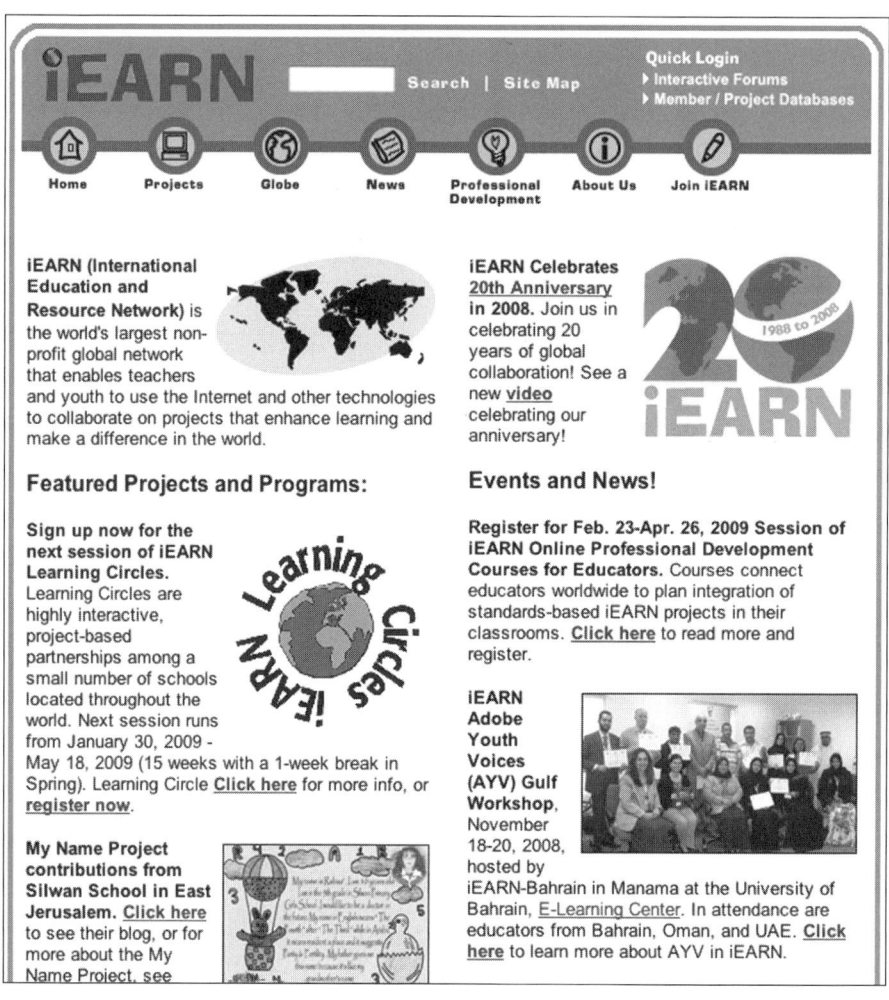

FIGURE 4.1 iEARN's homepage

What connects iEARN strongly with Célestin Freinet is its focus on decentralized decision making. iEARN is not a U.S.-dominated network; rather, it's governed through an assembly composed of one representative from each of the centers and a five-person executive board. A typical international project will involve a website set up by facilitators who are trained to help teachers collaborate and share lesson plans. The website (www.iearn.org, Fig. 4.1) serves to anchor the discussions and displays of student work.

HISTORICAL INTERLUDE

Célestin Freinet

Born in 1896 in a small French village close to the Italian border, Célestin Freinet was the founder of the education networking movement. Freinet's impoverished parents were unable to afford the fees to send him to a secondary school. After serving in the First World War and suffering a lung injury that prevented him from raising his voice and lacking a college or high school degree, he managed to find a job teaching in a local rural primary school. Minimizing the use of his voice led to the creation of a student-centered classroom. Through the use of a primitive printing press, his students produced a school newspaper, *Le Journal Scolaire (School Journal)*, and a class journal, *Livre de Vie (Book of Life)*.

Freinet soon met René Daniel, a fellow teacher from a neighboring province, and Freinet's approach took off when the two agreed to have their classes exchange "culture packages" filled with maps, photos, student writing, and local artifacts. The structure of exchange that Freinet and Daniel established in the 1920s laid the foundations of practices now followed by iEARN and other school networking sites.

The work of Freinet and Daniel was later expanded with the creation of clusters, consisting of several school partnerships all matched for age and curriculum interest, that included sending sample projects back and forth using the postal service as the means of communication. These exchanges included collaborative writing using the printing press that had been the foundation of Freinet's classroom approach. The partnerships were formalized in 1928 as the Public Educators' Co-operative (La Coopérative de L'Enseignement Laïc, CEL), and included other emerging technologies such as movies and tape recordings.

From these beginnings grew a network that extended to 10,000 schools around the world. As a tribute to Freinet's influence, teachers in France today can send parcels free of charge as long as they serve an educational purpose. Followers such as the Italian educator Mario Lodi translated Freinet's message to Italian schools when he formed the Cooperative Education Movement in 1951 with schools around the world. Al Rogers (1999) has translated some of Freinet's writings:

> Around the classroom, pupils are busily and excitedly writing. The content of their writing varies, but much of it is about their own personal adventures, the incidents that they have experienced inside and outside the classroom. From time to time they gather into groups to discuss, correct and edit one another's writing. After one or several revisions, the children print out their texts. Sometimes they assemble these texts to create a Class Journal or School Newspaper. Finally, the students gather their various writings together and send it off to other classes in other cities and towns, across the nation and around the world. In turn, they are just as excited to read … and re-read … the texts they have received in exchange from their partner classes. (1999)

These stories are not unlike what can be seen in many of today's cooperative learning classrooms. The leading global networks draw considerably from this early work when students share writing and research with peers in distant locations. The Learning Circles format developed by Margaret Riel, a key architect of AT&T and iEARN's approach, is quite similar to the cooperative learning strategies employed by Freinet: utilizing the writing, editing, and sharing of a common publication around a theme that is common to the participating classrooms. Riel (2006) writes in her teacher guidance:

> Many interesting projects in classrooms fail to make a lasting impression on students because the time was not taken to look back and review what was learned. The Circle publication plays a critical role in motivating students to organize and evaluate the information that they received from other students. Adults have a sense of the whole task from the beginning and can often anticipate the overall structure. For students, the project unfolds slowly, and early messages are often forgotten as they proceed to the end.

Analyzing Project Information

Each class organizes the information they received for their sponsored project into a section for the Circle publication. This process will help them learn how to review, summarize, evaluate and arrange information. Preparing the information for other participants in their Learning Circle and for parents and educators who will read their Circle publication gives students a clearly defined purpose and audience for their writing.

Your students' contributions to the other projects give them a very personal reason for wanting to read the work of their partner classrooms. In this way they will benefit directly from the educational activities that took place in the distant classrooms.

To be fair, the global dimension was less important than the notion of providing students with a sense of an authentic audience and purpose. But the notion of connecting students with a wider world was clearly embedded in the logic of the work of Freinet and his colleagues. They were clearly the vanguard and the foundation of the design of AT&T *Learning Networks* and their progeny. See the article "The Origins of a Global Network," by Al Rogers: http://gsh.lightspan.com/gsh/teach/articles/origins.htm.

I am indebted to Brave New Schools: Challenging Cultural Illiteracy through Global Learning Networks, *Cummins, Jim and Sayers, Dennis (Macmillan, 1995), the first book to highlight Celestin Freinet's significance in K–12 integration of global connections to the attention of an English-speaking audience.*

The Founding of iEARN

iEARN is the brainchild of educator Peter Copen, the current president of the Copen Family Fund. Copen is a former Westchester school teacher and founder/director of and teacher for the Walkabout Program, an alternative high school for juniors and seniors that used experiential learning in the form of community service, internships, academics, and backpacking to enrich young people's lives.

Copen wanted to use his experience as a progressive educator to make a difference in young people's lives. At the height of Cold War tensions, he conceived a telecommunications connection between 12 schools located in what was then the Soviet Union and 12 New York state schools. The five-year pilot project, funded by the specially created Copen Family Foundation, began as a research project to test the educational changes that would occur between a test and a control group.

Twelve schools in both countries taught English and Russian and used the then-emerging technologies of e-mail and video telephone. The fledgling connection not only improved language skills, but also deepened students' understanding of international and cultural issues, increasing their motivation to read authors from each other's countries and enriching the discussion of political and social issues. The continuing success of the project, in terms of changes in teachers' and students' lives after the first five years, is documented in "The New York State–Moscow Schools Telecommunications Project: The Founding Project of iEARN," (Bush, 2007). The report describes the lasting impact that the program had on teachers, students, and administrators.

iEARN Expands

Based on the success of the initial pilot project, Copen believed that the project should be expanded. He noted, "This is not only about education; it's about saving the world and the role that education can play in it." At international conferences and meetings, he met with volunteers who could launch iEARN networks in their own countries, using strategies that could work best to establish the idea of international collaborative school networking. Beginning with seven countries that had either established networks that were centralized around the Ministry of Education or decentralized in one or two cities in a country, the network founders were faced with a choice of whether to spend resources deepening the networks in each country or reaching out to include more countries.

> "The process of connecting through technology to the world has to be separated between the experience of the U.S. and the experience of the rest of the world. In any other country, they don't have global studies because it is second nature that their lives every day are impacted by the rest of the world, and they are connected to the world."
>
> *Ed Gragert, U.S. iEARN coordinator*

During the 1990s, following the break up of the Soviet Union, iEARN personnel decided to continue to embrace growth. With the assistance of the George Soros Open Society Institute, 25 new countries were recruited for the project between 1994 and 1996. African countries also were brought into the network during the 1990s as new excitement emerged about the possibilities of using technology to transform the African education systems.

During this period, Ed Gragert was appointed as U.S. director of iEARN. His formative experience began as a 17-year-old who decided to take a year between school and university, living with a South Korean family when he was just a teenager.

> I got off an airplane in Seoul, Korea, when I was 17 and spent a year in that country, living with a wonderful Korean host family and attending a Korean high school. This experience opened my eyes to new horizons and enabled me to view my own country from an external perspective. This year affected my decision to go into international education issues and to enable other American young people to experience the world.

Gragert was soon directing a student exchange program and working for a year on the Foreign Relations Committee. When he joined iEARN Gragert was confronted with the challenge of how to prepare teachers to collaborate. A key challenge for Gragert was to understand what was needed in terms of professional development. Careful observation of the early years of iEARN's growth convinced him that a one-size-fits-all, cookie-cutter approach could not work. Teacher training institutions typically avoided the subject of teacher collaboration, even between the classroom teacher down the hall, let alone a teacher in another country. He believed that each country should develop its own methodologies and resources, based on the fact that in many countries schools only had one computer, often located in the principal's office. In many regions, the only access to Internet computers was in cybercafes. As a result of Gragert's decisions, iEARN started to grow as a decentralized, loosely connected network open to all technologies from the postal service to high-speed videoconferencing.

When September 11, 2001 occurred, Gragert's network was poised to take a leadership role. iEARN was invited by the U.S. Department of Education to form a large coalition group capable of helping U.S. students better understand the changing world. The U.S. State Department assisted in providing professional development resources for 25 countries, many of them located in the Muslim world. One popular type of professional development emerged during this period. It utilized an asynchronous online format, with each course "divided into eight modules (one lesson per week) with readings, discussions, individual and group assignments. Lessons and assignments take participants step-by-step through the process of integrating an online collaborative project into their classroom" (www.iearn.org/professional/online.html/#offerings). University credits began to be recognized by several states.

The iEARN network continues to expand from 85 countries in 2001 to 120 countries in 2007. In the United States, 2,000 schools are members of the 25,000 worldwide member base, with 2 million students logging on to iEARN every day.

iEARN Project: De Orilla a Orilla

One of the first global learning networks explicitly influenced by Freinet's work is the *De Orilla a Orilla* (Spanish for "from shore to shore") network. Based in Puerto Rico, it is currently a member of iEARN. Founded in 1984, Orillas (as they are known) acknowledge the influence of Freinet—the intent of those who developed the Orillas was to:

> promote and extend an educational networking model first developed by the French educators Célestin and Elise Freinet in 1924. Following the Freinet model, Orillas is not a student-to-student pen pal project, but rather clusters of class-to-class collaborations designed by two or more partner teachers who have been matched according to common teaching interests and their students' grade level.
>
> *(Cummins, 1994, p. 300)*

Praise for the network and its pedagogy has been lavish—Robert DeVillar and Chris Faltis (2001, p. 116) judged Orillas "certainly one of the more, if not the most, innovative and pedagogically complete computer-supported writing projects involving students across distances." Cummins and Sayers (1995, p. 23) remark that "Orillas remains—after more than a decade—the leading global learning network project working to explore and expand the theoretical and practical boundaries of multilingual, intercultural learning."

The Orillas network's distinctiveness is grounded in establishing

> long-distance team-teaching partnerships between pairs or groups of teachers separated by distance, forming "sister" or "partner" classes with a focus that is both multinational and multilingual (including Spanish, English, French, Portuguese, Haitian, American, and French Canadian Sign Languages). Collaborating teachers make use of electronic mail and computer-based conferencing to plan and implement comparative learning projects between their distant partner classes. Such parallel projects include dual community surveys, joint math and science investigations, twinned geography projects, and comparative oral history and folklore studies. Often teachers in Orillas electronically publish their students' work over the Internet.
>
> *(Cummins & Sayers, 1995, p. 22)*

iEARN Project: Feeding Minds Fighting Hunger

The iEARN site on world hunger was launched on World Food Day 2000. Feeding Minds Fighting Hunger consists of ten international partners and nonprofit organizations, with a lead from the Food and Agriculture Organization (FAO) of the United Nations, and the U.S. National Committee for World Food Day. The program introduction includes the following guidance for teachers:

> Intended for use by teachers around the world, three easy-to-introduce teaching modules have been developed for use by each of three levels of education—primary, intermediate, and secondary—all of which cover, in varying degrees of complexity, the topics of What Are Hunger and Malnutrition? Who Is Malnourished? Why Is There Hunger in the World? and What Can We Do to Help End Hunger and Malnutrition? Background information and additional resources are provided to assist teachers in studying these topics with their students. Teachers around the world adapt and refine the materials, as necessary, to meet local needs and conditions.

> The lessons and teaching materials are available in Arabic, Chinese, English, Farsi, French, Greek, Bahamas Indonesian, Italian, Japanese, Portuguese, Russian, Spanish, and Kiswahili on CD-ROM, in print form upon request, and on the Internet at www.feedingminds.org. The website provides a forum through which teachers and students around the world can talk with each other and exchange ideas and experiences on these issues. Feeding Minds also reaches out directly to youth through its "Youth Window," which provides information, resources and activities for young people to use on their own. Providing additional information not included in the main Feeding Minds lessons, the "Youth Window" aims to interest and motivate teens inside or outside the classroom to join in global efforts to end hunger and malnutrition.

Evaluating iEARN

An evaluation of iEARN stressed that it helps students not only develop awareness of other cultures but deepens their appreciation for their own culture and increases compassion. It also helps students connect local problems with global challenges. In individual interviews, Peter Copen, teachers, and students consistently discussed the benefits of connecting across countries and cultures. One teacher from Romania said,

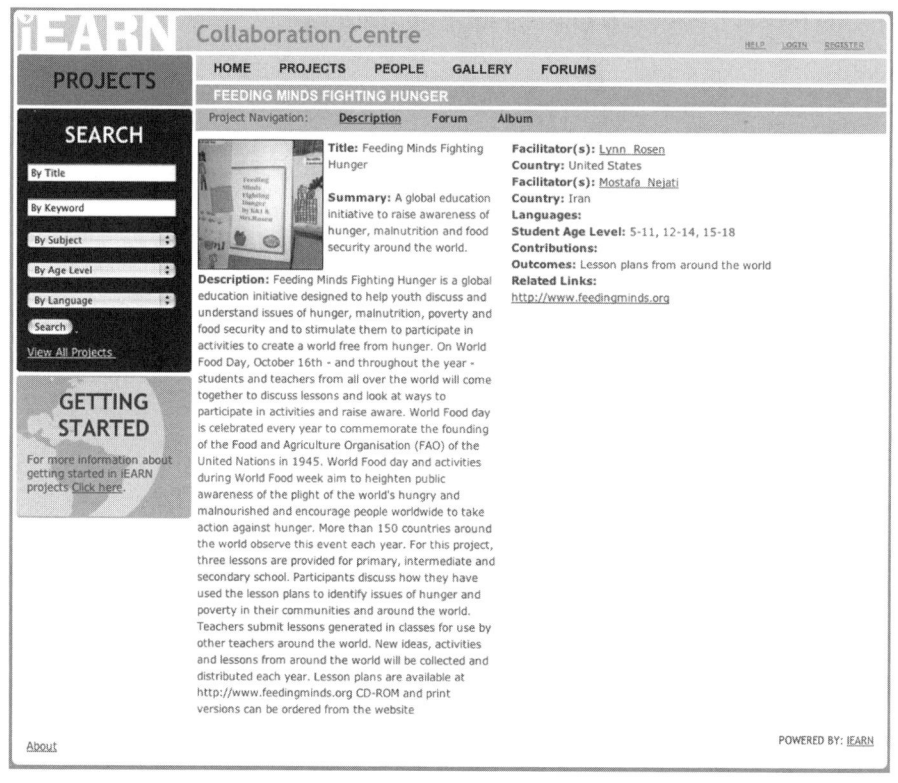

FIGURE 4.2 The Feeding Minds Fighting Hunger iEARN project.

"The most important thing about iEARN for me was the opportunity to make my students more aware of the culture and traditions we have and to share our culture and traditions with other students around the world" (Copen, 2002, p. 9). The report continues,

> Three out of four teachers (75%) said that iEARN helped their students appreciate other cultures very much. Sixty-one percent noted similar improvements in students' ability to make connections between local and global problems. In addition, 56% of teachers said that iEARN helped students feel more compassionate toward other people very much. Finally, approximately half of the teachers (53%) and students (49%) said that iEARN has helped students very much in their capacity to feel pride in their own culture. (p. 29)

A teacher from Taiwan said in her survey, "iEARN is a human network with each member of this family forming a home for global collaboration" (p. 10). According to the data, most iEARN students are collaborating with other students in their class or with students in other countries one to three times per month or four or more times per month. Seventy-eight percent of teachers reported that students collaborate on iEARN projects with other students in the same class.

5

Global Schoolhouse and Other Global Education Networks

There are many other highly successful global education networks. In this chapter we'll explore just a few of them.

Global Schoolhouse

Another successful global collaborative network, Global Schoolhouse, was launched in 1984 as the Free Educational Mail (FrEdMail) Network. Two San Diego teachers linked students on the West and East Coasts to participate in online writing projects. With a 1992 grant from the National Science Foundation, the group created its first website, called the Global Schoolhouse Network (GSN), to showcase online collaborative learning. According to their website (www.globalschoolnet.org), the mission of the GSN is "to provide a living curriculum that makes the world a laboratory and promotes the quest for lifelong learning."

With a far less elaborate procedure to engage with projects than iEARN, the GSN project began by connecting schools in California, Virginia, Tennessee, and London. "Learning clusters were formed consisting of four to six schools [whose students] worked as collaborative teams to study ground water pollution, solid waste management, alternative energy sources, space exploration, natural disasters, and weather" (www.globalschoolnet.org). The project established a global online network of educators who wanted to transform the way students learn and interact with one another and their communities.

FIGURE 5.1 The Global Schoolhouse operates the Global SchoolNet website.

Global Schoolhouse Project: A day at my school

By Ling-yun

Dates: 09/02/08 to 12/02/08

Ages: 10 to 15

Project Level: Basic Project

Curriculum Areas: Arts, Information Technology, International Relations, Language, Social Studies

Technology Types: Audio: files, clips, CDs, tapes; blogs; FTP [file protocol transfer]

Graphics: photo, draw, paint; Desktop Document Sharing

Text: stories, essays, letters

Video: files, clips, CDs, tapes

Collaboration Types: Information Exchange; Intercultural Exchange; Information Search; Peer Feedback

Sample Project Summary:

> Hello! I'm from Taiwan and now I'm planning a project called "A day at my school." I build up a blog at http://sampleblog.com. This blog is going to be the platform where students can share their school lives and any issues happening in the school. I hope students, with the teacher's help, have the chance to decide the topics and post related information on the blog (texts, pictures and even videos!), and then invite other students to give comments on the posted information on the blog. I turn the content of blog into a newspaper and mail to our learning partners! So we hope our partners can: 1. log onto the blog and discuss the topics of their school lives. If not, we still can try e-mails then post them on the blog. 2. e-mail us or work on the blog at least twice a month. Here I have 6 six students (fifth graders) in the learning project. We can speak and write Chinese and English. If you have interest, and want to know more detail, please let me know!

FIGURE 5.2 Example of a Global Schoolhouse project.

Global Schoolhouse provides an even easier entry point for the novice teacher than iEARN because there are some ready-made projects that involve flexible time commitments—as much or as little time as the teacher can afford to devote to the project.

Here's an example: Colorful Classrooms at www.globalschoolnet.org/gsh/pr/ GetDetail.cfm?StartRow=1&view=1&projtype=future%2Ccurrent%3Bopen&sortby= Start%20Date&fAge=5&tAge=19&pID=2819/.

This project requires that students "create a virtual book according to the Education for All Ideals of UNESCO. It is easy to participate: just send texts and illustrations concerning a day in school."

The Global Schoolhouse project offers topics that naturally excite students—such as sharing books with other students from around the world in a kind of virtual book club: www.globalschoolnet.org/gsh/pr/GetDetail.cfm?StartRow=21&view=1&projtype =future%2Ccurrent%3Bopen&sortby=Start%20Date&fAge=5&tAge=19&pID=3388/.

Or, tracking with other students what was happening around the world on the day they were born: www.globalschoolnet.org/gsh/pr/GetDetail.cfm?StartRow=21&view=1 &projtype=future%2Ccurrent%3Bopen&sortby=Start%20Date&fAge=5&tAge= 19&pID=564/.

Here's another: Helping the planet through projects with other schools to plant trees (The Green Wave) or requesting that students and faculty carpool for Earth Day: www.globalschoolnet.org/gsh/pr/GetDetail.cfm?StartRow=41&view=1&projtype= future%2Ccurrent%3Bopen&sortby=Start%20Date&fAge=5&tAge=19&pID=3029/.

Global Schoolhouse projects do not require iEARN's specially trained facilitators. Rather, the projects are designed as teacher-to-teacher collaboratives, and the projects are neither as demanding of time or as complex as most of the iEARN projects and can run for short as well as longer time periods.

ePals

In 1995, Tim DiScipio, a U.S. web entrepreneur, and his Canadian business partner, John Irving, thought up the idea for ePals as a way to allow students to find "pen pals" on the web, just as he had found a pen pal during his school days.

The partners started the project as a hobby, dedicating some spare servers in the back office while they serviced their large corporate clients' websites. The project began to grow after Tim first "seeded" some enterprising teachers and schools in the UK, Canada, France, and the United States to start their own partnerships. Word of mouth

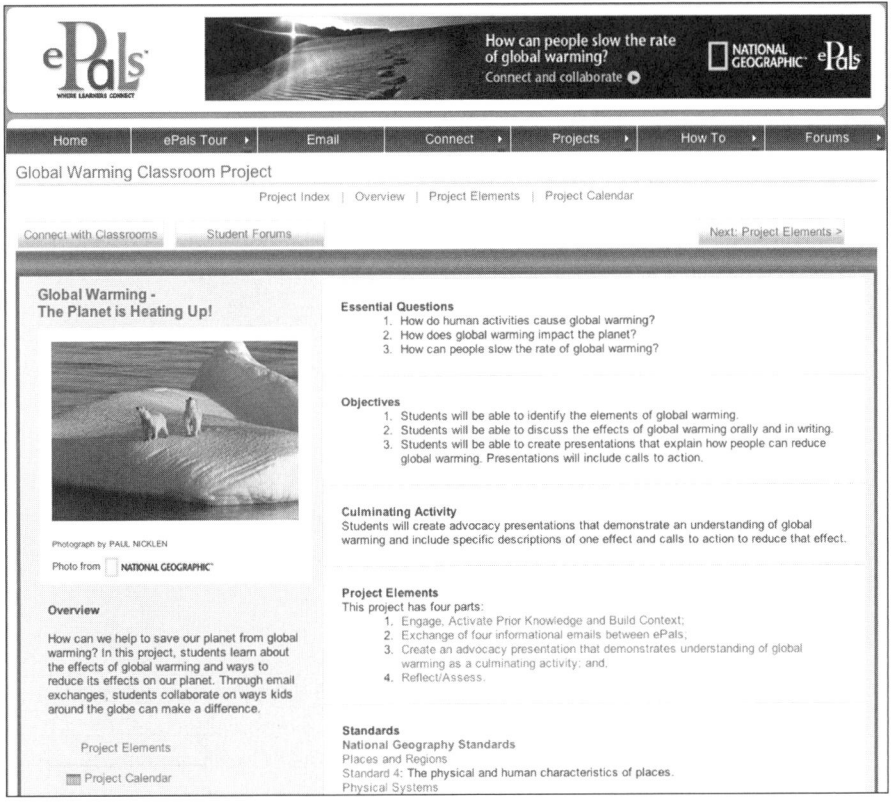

FIGURE 5.3 An ePals project list.

grew ePals to 13 million teachers and students in 200 countries and territories, with 1,000 new teachers registering each month from all over the world today.

One of the keys to ePals' success is that the site is secure, so students and parents do not have to worry about e-mail getting into unauthorized hands. It has an easy-to-use student- and teacher-friendly interface. ePals was the first site to integrate a translation tool, so communicating in most of the common Indo-European languages is no longer a barrier.

The site immediately appealed to educators who realized that students were very enthusiastic about communicating with their ePals. Research supported what teachers were reporting: that the students cared more about their writing because they were writing to a real audience, so they spent extra time making sure what they said was correct. They were also more willing to do any extra research that a project required.

Dr. Susan Gersh, a professor at the City College of New York who has researched ePals, confirms these findings but adds that although the tools are easy to use and students love them, many teachers she meets during workshops still have not heard of ePals. Teachers also may face barriers to using ePals (and other such tools, for that matter). In about half the schools Gersh visits, ePals is blocked by closed networks, and a lot of energy has to be put into gaining special permission to unblock the site.

See ePals for a sample lesson plan:
http://content.epals.com/projects/info.aspx?DivID=GlobalWarming_overview
and a full list of other engaging lesson plans:
http://content.epals.com/projects/info.aspx?DivID=index

CASE STUDY

Interview with Accomplished Global Educator Kim Cofino

September 2008

Please tell us about yourself.

After nine years teaching overseas, I am currently in my second year as the 21st Century Literacy Specialist at the International School Bangkok, Thailand. Previously, I spent five years as Middle School Academic IT Coordinator at Munich International School in Germany, and two years as Middle School Technology Facilitator at Mont'Kiara International School in Kuala Lumpur, Malaysia.

My work is focused on helping core subject teachers utilize web 2.0 technologies in the classroom, to create a global and collaborative approach to learning. I enjoy working with my colleagues to design authentic and engaging international projects incorporating social networking, blogs, wikis, and podcasts, and whatever comes next! I reflect on my learning on my professional blog: http://mscofino.edublogs.org

How did you get started as a globally oriented educator?

As an international school teacher, it's difficult not to be globally oriented in my teaching and learning practice. Having worked in Munich, Germany; Kuala Lumpur, Malaysia; and now Bangkok, Thailand; I have had the pleasure of working with teachers, students, and parents from all over the globe. This international experience has definitely helped me realize how important it is to enable students to make global connections, to develop intercultural understanding and to learn how to collaborate with those who may have a different cultural, social, or economic background. These are the skills that are going to be critical when they enter the workforce.

Describe some of the key stages in your development.

During the summer of 2006, I read Will Richardson's book, Blogs, Wikis, Podcasts, and Other Powerful Web Tools for Classrooms. *It was so inspiring and practical that as soon as I returned to my school in Kuala Lumpur, I began blogging with my students and set up my own professional blog. Later that school year, I participated in the K12Online conference, an entirely online (and totally free) conference, where I was able to connect and communicate with other like-minded educators. Realizing that there were many teachers around the world with similar goals for their teaching practice, I set up an RSS reader and began avidly reading more and more blogs. Over time I discovered the many educational networks on the social networking site Ning, read quite a few more books, and started connecting on a personal level through Skype and Twitter with colleagues in both international and public schools.*

I recently presented on this topic in Doha, Qatar, as a consultant for Qatar Academy. You can find my presentation and my resources here: http://21stcenturyeducator.wikispaces.com.

I also wrote an article on how to get started for the European Council of International Schools Shortcuts Newsletter, which you can find here: www.ecis.org/e-mails/shortcutsMAY08.htm.

What have been the most successful global education tech projects you have been involved with?

Pre-Kindergarten

- *The Meaning of Friendship: Students as Authors via SmartBoards: Pre-kindergarten students collaborate to write their own interactive book about the meaning of friendship in their class.*

Kindergarten

- *Kindergarten Connections: Connecting Students via VoiceThread: Two kindergarten classes connect for learning using VoiceThread, blogs, wikis, and digital imagery to share and discuss topics from the curriculum.*

Grade 1

- *Small Moments: ESL Students Present via VoiceThread:* Students write and illustrate a "small moment" for narrating and posting later on a VoiceThread. Hopefully, we can get a collaboration going with some other Grade 1 ESL students so that we can share our stories and comment on each other's work.

Grade 2

- *World Village:* Two second grade classrooms are connecting on Ning to explore intercultural understanding and to learn about the different cultures we have represented in our classes. The goal is to merge our two classrooms into one global village by conducting joint activities or projects once a month. We are going to focus on intercultural understanding and making connections between our different lifestyles.

Grade 4

- *1001 Flat World Tales: Collaborative writing using wikis:* Students will collaborate with other students in 12 classrooms around the world to produce exciting and unique persuasive writing enhanced with multimedia.

- *The Connected Classroom: Social Networking via Ning:* Eight international and local fourth-grade classrooms are connecting on one Ning to teach and learn from each other. Students will share screencasts of classroom learning, digital stories, more book reviews, student-led forum discussions, and whatever else comes up. The goal is to connect students on a personal level, in a private and safe space, to begin learning from each other, teaching each other, and collaborating on projects together. This is a year-long, always-on, global classroom.

- *Books Go Global! Developing a love of reading via VoiceThread and wikis:* Eight fourth-grade classes around the world use VoiceThread to get them excited about their next big project. They are going to create book reviews on VoiceThread (inspired by Wes Fryer's son, Alexander) and then will share them with partner schools around the world so that their single book review can become a dynamic conversation around books.

How do you measure their effectiveness with students?

Certainly engagement and motivation are indications of success, as well as achievement in the specified project goals.

What is some advice you would give to teachers starting out?

Model, model, model!

Teachers sometimes have a tendency to expect that as soon as students are given access to a technology tool, they will automatically know how to behave and interact with others. However, just because they can navigate the page and learn the tool quicker and easier (in most cases) than the teacher can upon first sight, doesn't mean that they know what to do once they get there.

All too often, teachers set up an online space for their students and then just "let them have a go"—basically leaving the students on their own in this new environment (sometimes because the teacher is not sure where to start). Not only does this provide fertile breeding ground for misbehavior, but it is definitely not something teachers would do in the physical world, so there's no rationale for "letting them go" in a virtual environment. Teachers must be the model for appropriate behavior online, just like they are in the physical classroom.

Once you have the groundwork laid—planning is done, international connections are made, teachers know the basics of the technology tools, students are members of the space—and you're ready to start working with the Ning, the first step is for the teachers (all of the teachers involved) to model appropriate use of the network. Teachers must model everything from behavior, to attitude, to quality of comments, to spelling and grammar, to appropriate use of the variety of features available. Yes, this is a lot of work. Yes, this will seem a bit teacher-focused in the beginning. Yes, this often requires teachers to check in on the network outside of school hours. But, I promise, in the end it will all be worth it. Once students have been given a clear model for how to interact in this environment, they will be able to move forward and develop on their own.

We're still in the initial phases of all of these projects, but I've gotten lots of positive feedback from parents and students already. They are enjoying the freedom to communicate and discuss their learning outside class hours and the opportunity to connect with other students around the world—exactly the same things I was excited about when I started exploring social networking last year. I can't wait to see how far we can go with this new tool!

What are some pitfalls to avoid?

When developing globally collaborative projects, the key is to be clear and consistent in your communication by developing specific and explicit expectations for all teachers. It is all too easy to plan a fabulous project only to find out that you intend to dedicate all your class time to the task while your teaching "partner" is asking his or her students to complete it for homework. Keeping the lines of communication open is key to ensure that all teacher facilitators have the same level of commitment and time in mind.

A helpful blog post on this topic: http://mscofino.edublogs.org/2007/12/20/a-step-by-step-guide-to-global-collaborations

Some further thoughts on social networking in the classroom: http://mscofino.edublogs.org/2007/12/22/making-connections-social-networking-in-the-elementary-classroom

Another helpful blog post is: http://mscofino.edublogs.org/2008/04/02/the-21st-century-educator

Many Other Opportunities Await!

A project in the Netherlands entitled Science Across the World gives students the latitude to explore topics like global warming and biodiversity in collaboration with groups of students from a database of schools. It's now a network of 5,269 teachers in 130 countries, using multiple languages with translations provided by a dedicated group of teachers. The Science Across the World website (www.scienceacross.org) provides an attractive gateway to varied and challenging international collaborations for students ages 10 through 16 (Figure 5.4).

Organizations like the National Aeronautics and Space Administration (NASA), the Discovery Channel, the Public Broadcasting Service (PBS), and a host of others offer high-quality video and interactive websites with a specific educational, rather than commercial, purpose. With the modularization of these applications, teachers can be more in control of the content and can develop a customized approach. The challenge to teachers is to sort through the hundreds of portals, video streaming sites, and websites that are available. The sponsoring organizations range from international ones that have enormous credibility, such as the United Nations Children's Fund (UNICEF) and the United Nations Educational, Scientific, and Cultural Organization (UNESCO), to organizations that do not hide the fact that they are commercial entities.

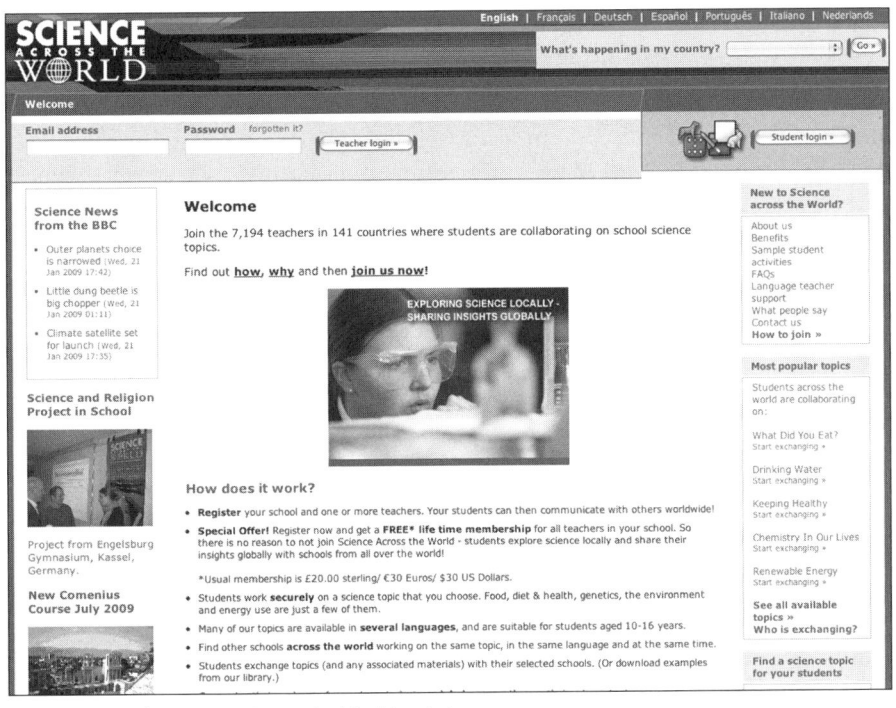

Global Schoolhouse and Other Global Education Networks • Chapter 5

FIGURE 5.4 The Science Across the World website.

Sites like TakingITGlobal (www.tigweb.org) are organized for students in school settings and in independent learning situations (Figure 5.5). This site helps students to find inspiration and information and to get involved in improving their local and global communities. The site includes extensive topics for threaded discussions in multiple languages.

With NASA's Passport to Knowledge project, classes can virtually travel on field trips to the Brazilian rainforest, participate in space experiments, and, in effect, "look over the shoulders" of working scientists and astronauts (http://passporttoknowledge.com/main.html).

Students participating in NASA's Jason Project remotely explore the ocean floor from their classrooms through a robot operated by the Woods Hole Oceanographic Institute (www.jason.org).

As part of the NASA's Live from Antarctica project (http://quest.arc.nasa.gov/antarctica/teacherguide.html) students access scientific diaries and field journals to learn how scientists "lived, worked, and played" at the South Pole.

The Comenius Project (http://ec.europa.eu/education/lifelong-learning-programme/doc84_en.htm) was established by the European Commission (EC) to advance school partnerships. Because of the EC sponsorship, Comenius' mission is focused on "enhancing the European dimension of education." The goal is to make it possible for schools to find business and education partners to create training opportunities for their preservice and in-service teachers. For example, proposals have been accepted by consortia of schools and colleges throughout Europe for a course on best practices in teaching languages and mathematics. One group developed a proposed curriculum on European Human Rights for training preservice teachers.

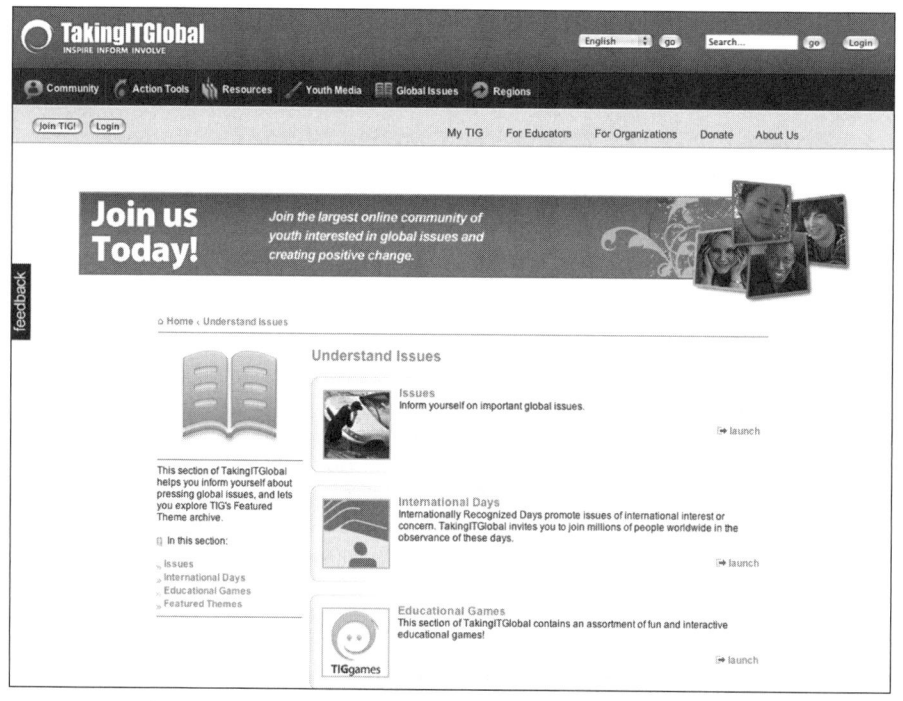

FIGURE 5.5 TakingITGlobal website.

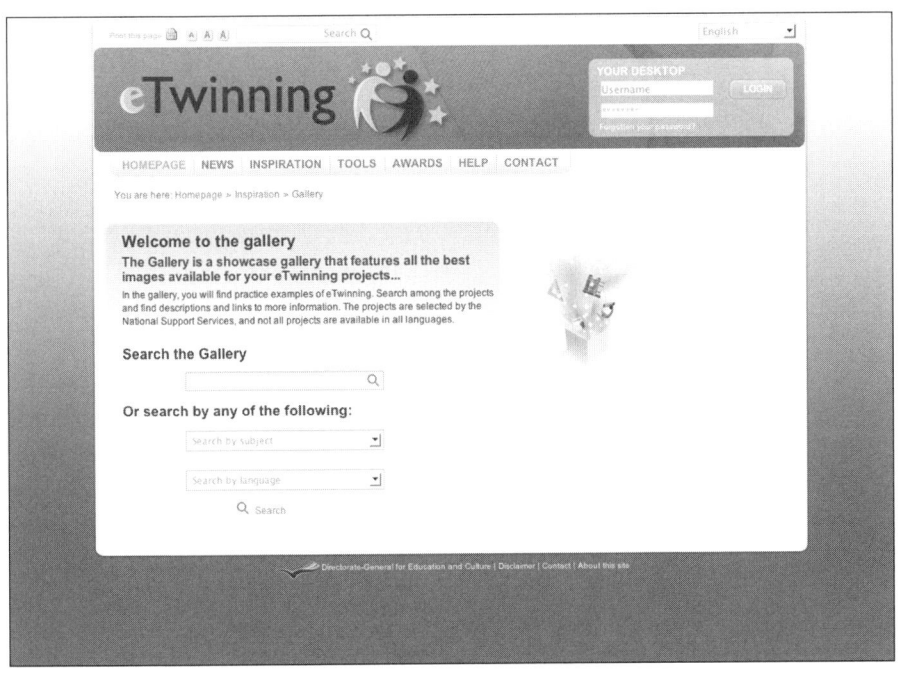

FIGURE 5.6 The eTwinning site connects schools in Europe.

The excellent eTwinning site (www.etwinning.net), is well-organized and full of ideas, suggestions, and ready-made project kits (Figure 5.6). This eTwinning program allows any European school to register and partner with another school on the basis of a subject or theme. The website is a model of its kind, offering new schools different options and ways of twinning. Begun in January 2005, it has attracted 13,000 schools. Each country has a team of people who are part of a National Support Service (NSS), and they are, in turn, supported by a Central Support Service (CSS) coordinated by the European Schoolnet, located in Brussels.

We are entering an exciting period of development, full of potential for educators interested in the use of these resources for accessing global perspectives. In the next chapter we'll take a look at the skills educators need to use these resources effectively, while staying consistent with appropriate educational standards.

6

Connecting Global Themes to Your Curriculum

As you've been reading, I bet one question may have been in the back of your mind: How do I integrate global perspectives into a K–12 standards-based curriculum?

Robert Hanvey's Foundational Essay

My recommendations are based on an important essay written by Robert Hanvey (1976), "An Attainable Global Perspective." His essay is widely regarded as foundational in the field of global education because he was one of the first to persuade educators that because we now inhabit an interdependent globalized community, it is not sufficient to simply be aware of the superficial differences between people. If we are to move beyond what Hanvey refers to as the "surface layer," we need to examine the unconscious assumptions we make about people who are different from us, people who have been socialized in a different way. By providing students with a variety of lenses to view the world, we are at the same time providing them with the tools and choices for creative problem-solving that are needed in a culturally diverse world with challenges and opportunities. To reach this deeper level of engagement, Hanvey calls for relevance in students' studies—including addressing world problems such as global warming, terrorism, and pandemics.

Hanvey outlines five basic dimensions for global perspectives that refocus students from being conscious of their own values and beliefs exclusively, to being aware that the world is composed of people with many different viewpoints that do not necessarily threaten their own. Students begin to realize that those perspectives not only exist, but deserve to be respected. A listing of the five dimensions follows:

1. *Perspective consciousness:* Awareness that each of us has a worldview, or "cognitive map," that is not universally shared by others and may be shaped by factors that we are unaware of and unable to control.

2. *Knowledge of world conditions* (also called "state-of-the-planet awareness"): Knowledge of prevailing and emergent world conditions, including population growth, migration, economic conditions, natural resources, and physical environment; political developments, science and technology, law, health, and international and intranational conflicts.

3. *Cross-cultural awareness:* Respect for and knowledge of the differing ideas, values, and practices found in human societies throughout the world.

4. *Knowledge of global dynamics:* Understanding how the world works and, in particular, understanding the key features and mechanisms of various global systems (e.g., cultural economic, political, ecological, and social).

5. *Knowledge of alternatives* (also called "awareness of human choices"): Awareness of alternatives to practices like unrestrained economic growth, current foreign aid/technical assistance policies, and existing consumption patterns.

Hanvey's five dimensions provide a useful framework for teachers who are exploring or expanding global learning. Most importantly Hanvey's scheme understands the ways that the developmental stages of young children, from solipsism—their view that the world they see around them is the only one—toward a respect and understanding of others, can move finally to a mature engagement with real world issues and choices.

Dimension One: Perspective Consciousness

The goal of dimension one is to help make students aware that not everyone shares their points of view. This is a first and basic step on the road to self awareness, a developmental stage that everyone must experience. A student may realize, for example, that her country is not perfect and that there may be something to learn from the problem-solving approaches taken by another nation. It may seem like an elementary step, but I have found that if students are not forced to challenge their own lack of knowledge and prejudices at critical junctures in their development, the opportunity may be lost.

Integrating Technology with Dimension One

- Examine an important national issue from the viewpoint of another country—how did different countries cover events in the Middle East? Hurricane Katrina? The U.S. elections? Using newspaper and media sources taken from a search on Google News (http://ncws.googlc.com) focus on an issue in the news that students are familiar with and have students role-play people from other countries.

- Join a series of video conference discussions where schools in different countries are linked together, such as those organized by Global Nomads, on a topical issue. Have students note the different approaches and assumptions of the different participants.

Dimension Two: Knowledge of World Conditions

Dimension two encourages the realization that the conditions students see around them may not universally prevail—that most people in the world live their lives where they were born, lead the same lives as their parents and grandparents, and the mobility that many people in advanced western societies have is a recent phenomenon.

Integrating Technology with Dimension Two

- Use a service like ePals to interview students concerning their physical and economic environment. Have students produce presentations such as blogs, wikis, or podcasts that illustrate a problem faced by the community they study.

- Focus on one local problem with global repercussions, such as recycling, or use of low-energy light bulbs.

Dimension Three: Cross-cultural Awareness

A good way to explain dimension three to American students is to contrast stereotypical American virtues of independence and self-reliance with the many cultures around the world that value group harmony, reciprocal relationships, and extended family.

Integrating Technology with Dimension Three

- Connect with classrooms located in countries where extended families are more the norm, such as Mexico and the Philippines, and have students survey each other concerning attitudes toward issues like the elderly, careers, customs, festivals, and so on.

- Using the previous classroom connections, compare classic short stories or folk tales and examine how they reflect qualities related to the value placed on extended families versus individual effort and achievement.

Dimension Four: Knowledge of Global Dynamics

The goal of dimension four is to make students aware of cultural interconnectedness from the viewpoint of unintended consequences of cultural exchange and influence. For example, trends that emerge in one culture may prove disruptive to another. Hanvey gives the example of a time when formula became more popular than breast-feeding in the West. This resulted in some unfortunate consequences when women in developing countries were encouraged to follow suit and ended up mixing formula with impure water.

Integrating Technology with Dimension Four

- Have your students and students from a classroom in another country each develop a list of cultural icons. Compare the lists to find the overlap and the differences. Discuss how each icon may represent each culture's values.

- Compare country-specific websites of globally branded companies and try to determine the differences and why they exist.

Dimension Five: Knowledge of Alternatives

Thanks to the recent attention given to global warming, our students probably better understand dimension five—the world as a system of interdependent parts—than students would have when Hanvey wrote the paper in 1976. But I wonder if they are as aware of the choices that other societies must make in regard to global warming? India recently introduced a car that is priced at $2,500, allowing millions of Indians to drive for the first time, causing untold additional pollution and likely increasing global warming. But how do you tell an Indian family they cannot have an affordable car?

Integrating Technology with Dimension Five

- Develop a mock UN or global treaty, such as Kyoto, with a collaborating classroom. Place on the discussion an item concerning a global problem—like HIV/AIDS, global warming, or terrorism. Have students take on the role of their country's envoy who must trade off or compromise on certain items in order to reach an agreement.

- Pair students off between collaborating classrooms and ask them to role-play international consultants who need to develop multimedia campaigns in each other's home country to help build public support for compromise around key issues with global impact.

Preparation Is Essential

One of the best ways to find a partner teacher is to look on any one of the major global teaching sites (Global Schoolhouse, iEARN, Global Classrooms, ePals, KidLink). These sites all have bulletin boards for teachers looking for international partners. Your first step is to e-mail in response to project postings you find interesting or to post your own project.

Global collaborative work with a partner teacher using web 2.0 technologies takes some preliminary effort to prepare. For a first collaboration, I would recommend allowing up to six weeks for preparation. Assignments should be aligned so that they fit within each teacher's curriculum goals and so that the assessment rubrics reflect the relevant standards and objectives. If synchronous conversations—which are ideal for students to get to know their counterpart well—are to be attempted, special arrangements often need to be in place, with the classes arranging at least one **virtual meeting** before or after school.

All this initial effort can seem like a lot of work, yet the reason to persist is that it can have a huge payoff. Beyond the bond forged between schools possibly thousands of miles away from one another, lasting friendships often form, as many of the global teachers I spoke with mentioned them. The award-winning teachers I interviewed for this book routinely talked about the partner school becoming part of their own community—U.S. teacher Ann Lambert, for example, reflects that after communicating with students located in Africa, she felt like they were only "about a block away, somewhere in the canyons where we couldn't see them."

As you and your partner teacher develop mutual trust and confidence, you realize that you can also keep perfecting the lesson each year. You never know; you may also get an opportunity to visit your partner teacher, as many global teachers have managed to do as a result of their work.

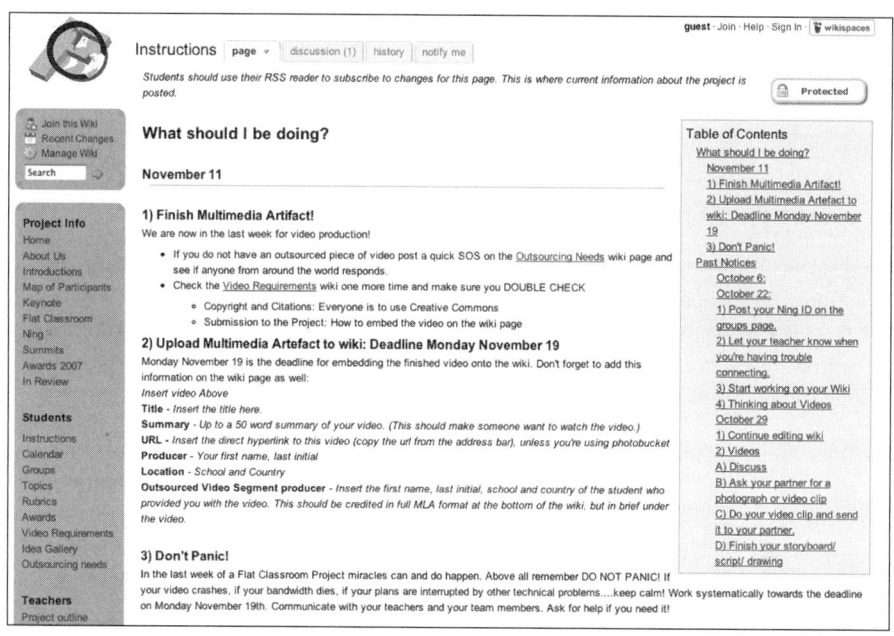

Chapter 6 • Connecting Global Themes to Your Curriculum

FIGURE 6.1 A wiki from the Flat Classroom Project.

All teachers are different in the ways they like to format lessons. In the area of global collaboration, there are some methods that may work better than others. I recommend teachers place the entire module (by this, I mean a series of linked lessons) online. You can easily do this by devoting a wiki—shared by both teachers and classrooms—to the lesson plan and relevant resources. The advantages of doing this are enormous: you can show your students the meaning of collaboration, and you can also let students know on a daily or even hourly basis how they are performing. Students can work at their own pace through the materials without your active intervention, and they also know that everything they do with the wiki is documented. The wiki can be subdivided so that there is a space for teacher instructions from both teachers. A wiki example is shown in Figure 6.1 from Vicki Davis and Julie Lindsay of the Flat Classroom Project.

Sample Module Design

I recommend including the following elements in each module you create:

Warm-up activities should be designed as a standard way to focus students on a topic, beginning with the knowledge they have and building upon this foundation.

Introductory profiles should include the names of the participating students, student photos (optional, if permission is granted by parents to use on a secure site such as ePals), the interests of each student—hobbies, sports, favorite books, movies, heroes—and what each student hopes to learn by participating in the project.

Country research directs students to review information about the other country using a website like CountryWatch: www.countrywatch.com/youthedition/ or the CIA World Factbook: https://www.cia.gov/library/publications/the-world-factbook/.

A self-reflection blog allows students to write their thoughts and feelings down as they work through the unit. An advantage of blogging instead of traditional journals is the ability to link with websites and other materials—this ability can bring writing alive for students. A good platform to consider is the ePals platform SchoolBlog. Its features include searchable archives; personalized domains; multimedia postings; calendars; surveys; design templates; classroom-only, parents-only, and public access areas; web-based management and storage; rich text editor; manuals and tutorials; Google Docs; and spreadsheets. These features allow students to collaborate from any computer, including computers at home: www.epals.com/groups/about/pages/schoolblog.aspx.

Mapping directs students to find the counterpart school on a map. Consider using tools like National Geographic's Map Machine: http://maps.nationalgeographic.com/map-machine or Google Earth: http://earth.google.com.

Collaboration using a wiki. The wiki will house the lessons and directions, the work of both classrooms of students, resources, and assessments. There are many free wiki tools available. One often preferred by educators is Wikispaces because of its simplicity and lack of advertising: www.wikispaces.com/site/for/teachers/.

Multimedia content sharing tools

VoiceThread: This is an easy-to-use tool that will thoroughly engage students as it allows images to be placed in a slide show format that can be narrated as if you are telling a story aloud. The pro version is free to K–12 educators: http://voicethread.com.

Flickr: Students can easily share photographs, and they can choose to make them private or public: www.flickr.com.

ScrapBlog: This is similar to VoiceThread in that it allows users to assemble a multimedia scrapbook easily from text, video, audio, and photos: www.scrapblog.com.

Animoto: Students will enjoy creating their own videos from photos and adding music: http://animoto.com, and http://educatipon.animoto.com is aimed at educators.

OneTrueMedia: Another free multimedia uploading service: www.onetruemedia.com.

Assessment. Teachers should recognize the different nature of global collaborative work in the way they weight their grades—taking fully into account the group discussion work and the various ways students participate.

On the following page is a suggested template for a typical middle school or high school module that may be modified according to the way you adapt these lesson plans. I suggest forming a more detailed rubric for each assignment and placing it online using Rubistar (http://rubistar.4teachers.org/index.php).

Activity	Outline	How to Measure	Suggested Weight (%)
Participation in Group Discussions and Calendar Activity	A Highly sensitive and nuanced comments —ability to lead discussion in a positive way B Several sound comments but does not take initiative very often C Largely passive and not very sensitive to the nuances of the discussion, a few comments D Many unhelpful comments making it difficult for the group to function, an occasional sound comment	i) Teacher observation ii) Effort as it appears evident on the blog/wiki	20
Collaborative Group Presentation	A Highly creative use of the media material to apply cultural understandings to the content so that the material is highly readable/watchable and attuned to its audience B Some creativity and good understanding of the cultural issues but does not fully cohere—either because of poor editing or choice of materials C Routine performance that is only sporadically adjusted to the needs of its audience D Unable to complete the basics of the assignment but made some efforts	i) Quality of product ii) Student self-assessment report	35
Reflective Essay	A Exhibits a mature understanding of the way cultural differences work, and the writer supports the points made through careful reasoning and appropriate evidence B Some insights but includes errors and lack of support for some of the points made. This essay could be more persuasive. C Routine performance does not convince the reader that any but minimal learning has taken place D Lack of basic ability either to choose important points to write about or support points made but turned in an essay	i) Essay	45

7

Quick Ways to Get Started

Collaboration on a project with an international partner, while well worth it, can take weeks of preparation. Maybe you'd like to just jump in and get your feet wet. This chapter is designed to help you find entry points to globalize any topic and to do so in a way that engages students' interests. I also explore speedy ways to integrate global perspectives into the classroom that do not necessarily depend on extensive collaboration with an international partner classroom. The ideas are meant to inspire you to dive in and want to do more. I have grouped the ideas according to age range.

An ePals Activity for Elementary Students

There is some evidence that the earlier you introduce students to global awareness activities, the more impact they will have (Fiske, 2000; Galinsky & Moskowitz, 2000). For elementary students to believe that countries in the southern hemisphere experience different seasons from those in the north, communicating with their counterparts in the opposite hemisphere has a much deeper impact than simply being told about what seems like an imaginary place.

ePals hosts a captivating module for elementary students. Youngsters at this age are often fascinated with the Cinderella fairy tale. When they partner with an e-pal in another country and discover that the story is told differently in that country, the result is a strong motivator to describe the different nuances and to learn more about the ways that folk tales represent something important about another part of the world.

ePals supports these kinds of investigations through well-designed charts that help students organize questions and answers. See Figure 7.1 for example.

Cinderella Synopsis Instructions: Write a paragraph or two that describes the similarities and differences that you have found between your version and your student partner's version of this story. Use the Cinderella Chart below to help organize your information.		
Question	**Your Answer**	**Your Partner's Answer**
Story name		
Name of main character		
Family members		
Impossible jobs that she had to do		
Magic in story		
Animals that helped Cinderella		
How she proved her true identity		
Whom she loved		
What happened to evil characters		
How the story ended		

FIGURE 7.1 Cinderella Chart. *Source: www.epals.com/forums/p/9071/30805.aspx.*

Culminating activities provide students with an enjoyable range of activities to collaborate on, like searching the Internet for Cinderella stories. You might also prepare a **WebQuest** (a set of websites that are listed in a PowerPoint, like an online slide show). For this activity, have students indicate on a world map where in the world the stories originate.

A Virtual Tour Guide Activity for Middle School Students

One of my graduate students, Linda Labelle, designed a Virtual Tour to help her middle school students understand the symbolic function of landmarks. She asked her students to imagine that they were tour guides and to choose an international landmark that would be their topic for an interview with an international partner. Here are some of the questions Labelle asks her students to answer after interviewing student partners in other countries:

- What does your assigned landmark mean to the people of the host country?
- What did you learn through your research?
- What does this landmark symbolize to you after your research?
- What did you learn about understanding and acceptance of other people's beliefs?
- If you could, knowing what you know now, would you travel to your assigned landmark's host country?

Engaging Middle and High School Students with Current Events

> Today's youth are quite possibly the most media and technologically savvy generation there has ever been. It goes without saying that this degree of sophistication deserves an equally sophisticated—and creative—pedagogical approach. As a complement to traditional textbooks, GNG's (Global Nomads Group's) programs harness technology in a way that both arouses students' curiosity and puts them in charge of their own education.
>
> *Global Nomads website: www.gng.org*

Global Nomads allows students to be not simply spectators of world events, but to feel like they are a part of the news. They may join a videoconference with students living in a war zone or ask questions of experts about their views on news they have reported.

The programs serve to empower students. A typical Global Nomads program calls for each class participating in an international discussion to have its own moderator(s). The moderator is in charge of opening and closing statements and of making sure discussions run smoothly. Without any direct intervention from teachers or adults, students are encouraged to become true ambassadors for their countries or communities.

Global Nomads pairs schools ahead of time and provides participating classes with supporting reading material and videoconferencing scripts that delineate the structure of each event. They provide cues for moderators. The following list is from the Global Nomads website.

For each program, Global Nomads will provide participating schools with:

- A lesson plan and learning resources for students and teachers;
- Sample questions for students to ask in order to participate in the class;
- Advice on teaching with video conferencing and interactive media;
- Access to GNG's existing network of partner schools in the U.S. and in other countries;
- Sign-ups, scheduling, and coordination of students and schools;
- Facilitation of the videoconferences;
- Experts in relevant areas when appropriate;
- Post conference resources for students to learn more or to stay in contact with each other;
- Technical support.

CNN Students News (www.cnn.com/studentnews/) is geared toward K–12 learners, can provide students with a true sense of global stories, and includes useful quizzes and classroom exercises.

Newseum (www.newseum.org/todaysfrontpages/default.asp) contains newspaper front pages from 45 countries. The site can be made far more valuable if students are assigned the task of composing a set of world newspaper headlines from a review of 10 to 20 international newspapers. Or, ask them to make a comparison among the ways a story is covered by newspapers from different countries. The parent website (www.newseum.org) states they are "the world's most interactive museum."

Connecting Middle and High School Students with Their Passions

The quickest way to engage students is to allow them to research topics they are already passionate about, such as music or human rights. Here are a couple websites with excellent teacher-ready resources.

Some of the most exciting web 2.0 lesson plans I have found related to global music are on the Oxfam website (www.oxfam.org.uk/education/resources/global_music_lesson_plans). A set of five lesson plans includes informative and enjoyable activities that explore everything from improvising traditions of different cultures and styles, to how music is used to convey social, political, and cultural messages. Oxfam has also developed an entire K–12 curriculum for schools.

Amnesty International provides detailed lesson plans and resources for an entire range of human rights issues in the news (www.amnesty.org.au/hre/comments/2310). The site includes teacher guides and offers additional resources for teachers—many are ready-made single lesson plans or a series of plans and provide safe entry points for utilizing technology-based resources. These web-based lesson plans, movie clips, photos, and slides can help start a discussion or provide material for student essays or reports.

8

Final Thoughts

I'd like to share the views of three global education leaders that corroborate the basic premise of this book, that we must educate students to have a global perspective.

> U.S. high school graduates will: Sell to the world; buy from the world; work for international companies; manage employees from other cultures and countries; collaborate with people all over the world in joint ventures; compete with people on the other side of the world for jobs and markets; and tackle global problems, such as AIDS, avian flu, pollution, and disaster recovery.... We need to open global gateways and inspire students to explore beyond their national borders.
>
> *(Stewart, 2007, p. 8)*

> Globalization is a fact. Every major problem we face—from economic growth to the environment to public health to reducing poverty and inequality to improving national and homeland security will require more international knowledge and cooperation than ever before....
> If we are to have a world-class education system, and let's really talk about world-class, our definition of educational excellence must go

beyond literacy and numeracy to include knowledge of the history, geography, cultures, and languages of other parts of the world.

(Engler &Hunt, 2004, p. 8)

Global educators share certain characteristic instructional strategies: they confront stereotypes and exotica and resist simplification of other cultures and global issues; foster the habit of examining multiple perspectives; teach about power, discrimination, and injustice; and provide cross-cultural experiential learning.

(Merryfield, 2002)

Before leaving you with the idea that global collaboration is magically going to create excited and engaged students, raise their achievement levels, and—dare I say?—even move us closer to world peace, a few cautionary words are in order. It *is* extra work (coordinating time zones, lesson times, plans, and preparation); you may still be wondering whether it's worth all the extra effort. You may also suspect that some students do not share your excitement for global collaboration.

If you require praise from your colleagues or supervisors, global collaborations may not be a good investment of your time, because much of the work can remain hidden from administrators who often have no idea of what it takes to make such collaborations possible. You should also not begin a global collaboration just because of the "coolness factor"—students increasingly demand relevancy, especially older students. Sometimes our innovative efforts in the classroom fail and can seem like a waste, but we have to examine the reasons, for any new initiative takes time for both teachers and students to get used to. Clay Burrell, the founder of 1001 Flat Tales, offers sage advice for teachers: the goal should be to try to embed global collaboration into the classroom seamlessly, rather than drawing undue attention to it. Clay says, "Just model the stuff by using it, and let it sink in that way" (Burrell, 2008). Clay's advice is salient—as web 2.0 tools become more ubiquitous, easy to use, and part of students' everyday lives, global collaborations could become as easy as signing in onto their social networking site.

We need to engage in global collaborations. Students need to communicate directly with others on the planet, rather than consume information about diverse nations and cultures indirectly via a teacher, textbook, or video. Direct experience is at the source of many important lessons—lessons that inscribe themselves into our deeper selves.

The way we do business is changing. More than 40% of IBM's employees, for example, do not work in traditional offices—rather, they are in constant electronic touch with their coworkers around the world from home or while on the road. At many companies employee communications happen through blogs, wikis, instant messaging, videoconferencing, and other corporate-wide collaboration tools. In their book, *Wikinomics: How Mass Collaboration Changes Everything* (2006), authors Donald Tapscott and Anthony Williams discuss an interview with Steve Mills, who runs IBM's software operation. They observe how he was "immersed in twenty different instant messaging sessions with clients and colleagues around the world" (p. 30). Mills notes, "The whole world feels local to me. I don't need to be present in the room to participate" (p. 265). This is how business is done in the 21st century.

The Partnership for 21st Century Skills (www.21stcenturyskills.org)—a coalition of business and education policy leaders, ten states, and a variety of educational organizations—is beginning to define a new curriculum that meets the needs of students in a globally interconnected economy. Arizona, Iowa, Kansas, Maine, Massachusetts, New Jersey, North Carolina, South Dakota, West Virginia, and Wisconsin are pledging support for the new skills that will be needed. In Wisconsin, the state superintendent and governor convened a Statewide International Education Council in 2002 and recommended five key goals:

- Global Literacy. Wisconsin's citizens need to be globally literate to understand the linkage of economies, peoples, and cultures around the world, and to function comfortably and effectively in other languages and cultures.

- World languages for all students

- Global training for all teachers

- Intercultural experiences for all citizens

- International linkages for Wisconsin businesses and government

Similarly, an increasing number of schools are declaring themselves "global" or establishing year-long courses in global studies. Evanston Township High School in Illinois requires each sophomore to take a mandatory year in global studies that includes courses where students impersonate a typical individual from a chosen country. Also at Evanston, a digital autobiography project allows students to create digital autobiographies that are e-mailed to its sister school in Japan. At the Chinese American International School (CAIS) in San Francisco, students learn to operate a computer in Chinese, as well as in English, and then use their new skills to communicate and create presentations with international e-pals.

The stereotypical thinking that characterizes Americans in the post-9/11 world is examined by professor and former diplomat Akbar Ahmed (2007) in his book *Journey into Islam: The Crisis of Globalization*. Ahmed notes the Western media's tendency after 9/11 to view the world "simplistically through the lens of security, terrorism…. The unfavorable and marginal portrayal of Islam only further widens the chasm between the West and mainstream Muslims." He further notes that compounding the problem, "Many Americans live in a bubble consisting of the office, the supermarket, and their sections of town, where they are not necessarily forced to engage with people who are different from them—racially, ethnically, religiously, or economically." Ahmed argues persuasively that the United States must construct a new philosophy toward other civilizations that takes into account their complexities.

Americans are increasingly sorting themselves into "communities of sameness," says Bill Bishop (2008) in his book, *The Big Sort: Why the Clustering of Americans Is Tearing Us Apart*, addressing the social, cultural, and political consequences of segregation. When we live in such homogeneous communities, our perspective on the world inevitably narrows—we become more fearful of those who look different from us or who possess different viewpoints.

Throughout this book, I have suggested ways you can help your students become globally aware citizens. The projects you start with do not have to be heavy on technological sophistication. An entire team of creative, technology-savvy organizations, led by enterprising educators, realized the tremendous potential of the world wide web—including organizations like iEARN, ePals, Global Schoolhouse, and others—and have created the tools and the curriculum materials to help you help your students make global connections.

In the past, schools have been adept at screening out much of the world that exists beyond the classroom. If every teacher begins to see him or herself as a global teacher, infusing and integrating global understanding, we can rise to the challenge of helping our students gain the global perspective they will need.

So often we educators believe that as students develop, they need less emotional context to their studies, less personal connection with what they are learning. However, I suggest that the reverse can be true: By using technology to communicate with others around the world, we can help restore some of that missing emotional energy; we can help students to forge bonds and associations that go deeper than simply the knowledge we spend much time trying to squeeze into our allotted lesson plans. By allowing students to experience other cultures via communications with their peers in those cultures, their knowledge of facts deepens into greater understandings.

The generation that my own children are part of will need to understand more about what *unites* people across the planet than what *divides* them, if they are to solve problems effectively, including global warming, energy shortfalls, terrorism, and a host of other challenges. As teachers, we need to show our students that we are part of an interconnected planet.

9

Sample Lesson Plans

Cinderella Around the World

Adapted with permission from ePals lesson www.users.on.net/~wayne_r/lit/cinderella.htm.

Subjects language arts, reading

Grades 3–5

Summary
Students develop their understanding of how fairy tales originate and how they are modified over time and by different cultures by exploring with students of another country the popular tale of Cinderella.

Suggested time allowance five one-hour lessons.

RELEVANT STANDARDS

McREL LANGUAGE ARTS

READING

Standard 6. Uses reading skills and strategies to understand and interpret a variety of literary texts

Level II (Grades 3–5)

1. Uses reading skills and strategies to understand a variety of literary passages and texts (e.g., fairy tales, folktales, fiction, nonfiction, myths, poems, fables, fantasies, historical fiction, biographies, autobiographies, chapter books)

2. Knows the defining characteristics of a variety of literary forms and genres (e.g., fairy tales, folktales, fiction, nonfiction, myths, poems, fables, fantasies, historical fiction, biographies, autobiographies, chapter books)

NATIONAL EDUCATIONAL TECHNOLOGY STANDARDS FOR STUDENTS

2. **Communication and Collaboration**

Students use digital media and environments to communicate and work collaboratively, including at a distance, to support individual learning and contribute to the learning of others. Students:

  a. interact, collaborate, and publish with peers, experts, or others employing a variety of digital environments and media

  c. develop cultural understanding and global awareness by engaging with learners of other cultures

RESOURCES

Computers with Internet connection

ePals account for the teacher and each of the students (www.epals.com)

PREPARATION

1. Familiarize yourself with ePals (www.epals.com) and use its Connect feature to locate a partner classroom. For help, visit http://community.epals.com/content/ePalsSupport.aspx.

2. Familiarize students with ePals by taking the ePals Tour (http://community.epals.com/groups/about/pages/epals-overview.aspx). Have students create individual accounts and practice e-mailing each other.

3. Review netiquette and have students practice writing a variety of e-mail messages.

OBJECTIVES

- Students will recognize story elements in different versions of a fairy tale.

- Students will compare and contrast different versions of a fairy tale in e-mail collaborations and in an essay.

- Students will correspond and collaborate with students in another country using good etiquette.

ACTIVITIES

1. Divide up the classes in pairs, with each pair consisting of one student from each country, and have the students introduce themselves via e-mail.

2. Have each student pair read a classic version of the Cinderella story and one of the following 16 Cinderella story variations provided here: www.pitt.edu/~dash/type0510a.html, or allow the teacher from the partner classroom to provide the version of the Cinderella tale his or her students are most familiar with in their own country.

3. Student pairs then collaborate via e-mail to compare the two versions of the tale using the following topic headings to help organize the information.

    - Story name
    - Name of main character

- Family members
- Impossible jobs that main character had to do
- Magic in story
- Animals that helped main character
- How main character proved her true identity
- Whom the main character loved
- What happened to evil characters
- How the story ended

4. In class, students discuss the work they did with their partner and how they felt about the collaboration. Each student chooses his or her best two e-mails and responses and shares them.

5. Students individually write an essay about which version of the story they preferred (classic or international variation) and why.

6. Each student writes a new Cinderella story using the above elements and shares it with his or her international partner for feedback.

ASSESSMENTS

- Essay concerning which Cinderella version of the story students prefer (rubric: http://rubistar.4teachers.org/index.php?screen=PrintRubric&rubric_id=1638752&no_return=1&).
- Two best e-mail responses (rubric: http://rubistar.4teachers.org/index.php?screen=ShowRubric&rubric_id=1639147&).
- Cinderella story (rubric: http://rubistar.4teachers.org/index.php?screen=ShowRubric&rubric_id=1639150&).

EXTENSIONS

Have students tell their original Cinderella stories via a podcast, a VoiceThread, or a PowerPoint presentation, or have all students share their stories on a specially constructed ePals blog.

Do Food Choices Affect Global Warming?

Subjects geography, economics, English/language arts, global education

Grades 6–8

Summary
Students work to understand where their own food originates and subsequently collaborate with partners in another country to explore the question: How do our food choices affect global warming? Students create a multimedia presentation that presents their findings and recommends actions to combat global warming. Students write a reflective essay exploring whether their new knowledge might change their future behavior.

Suggested time allowance three one-hour lessons; one hour preparation time for each lesson.

RELEVANT STANDARDS

McREL GEOGRAPHY

PHYSICAL SYSTEMS

Standard 8. Understands the characteristics of ecosystems on Earth's surface

Level III (Grades 6–8)

2. Understands the functions and dynamics of ecosystems (e.g., interdependence of flora and fauna, the flow of energy and the cycling of energy, feeding levels and location of elements in the food chain).

McREL ECONOMICS

Standard 1. Understand that scarcity of productive resources requires choices that generate opportunity costs

Level III (Grades 6–8)

1. Understands that scarcity of resources necessitates choice at both the personal and the societal levels.

McREL LANGUAGE ARTS

Standard 1. Uses the general skills and strategies of the writing process

Level III (Grades 6–8)

3. Editing and Publishing: Uses a variety of strategies to edit and publish written work (e.g., eliminates slang; edits for grammar, punctuation, capitalization, and spelling at a developmentally appropriate level; proofreads using reference materials, word processor, and other resources; edits for clarity, word choice, and language usage; uses a word processor or other technology to publish written work).

4. Evaluates own and others' writing (e.g., applies criteria generated by self and others, uses self-assessment to set and achieve goals as a writer, participates in peer response groups).

5. Uses content, style, and structure (e.g., formal or informal language, genre, organization) appropriate for specific audiences (e.g., public, private) and purposes (e.g., to entertain, to influence, to inform).

NATIONAL EDUCATIONAL TECHNOLOGY STANDARDS FOR STUDENTS

2. **Communication and Collaboration**

    Students use digital media and environments to communicate and work collaboratively, including at a distance, to support individual learning and contribute to the learning of others. Students:

    a. interact, collaborate, and publish with peers, experts, or others employing a variety of digital environments and media

    b. communicate information and ideas effectively to multiple audiences using a variety of media and formats

    c. develop cultural understanding and global awareness by engaging with learners of other cultures

    d. contribute to project teams to produce original works or solve problems

THE AMERICAN FORUM ON THE HUMANITIES

Students should understand the issues related to agricultural and environmental sustainability as local and global issues.

GEOGRAPHY

Standard 14. Understands how human actions modify the physical environment

Topics 1. Impact of society on the environment; 2. Science, technology, and society; 3. Environmental issues

Level III (Grades 6–8)

Benchmark 4. Understands the environmental consequences of both the unintended and intended outcomes of major technological changes in human history (e.g., the effects of automobiles using fossil fuels, nuclear power plants creating the problem of nuclear-waste storage, the use of steel-tipped plows or the expansion of the amount of land brought into agriculture)

RESOURCES

Computers with Internet connection and PowerPoint

ePals accounts for the teacher and each of the students (www.epals.com)

PREPARATION

1. Break the students into groups of four and ask each of the groups to choose a typical meal and bring in labels from the foods represented in that meal.

2. Familiarize yourself with ePals and use its Connect feature to locate a partner classroom (www.epals.com). For help, visit http://community.epals.com/content/ePalsSupport.aspx.

3. Familiarize students with ePals by taking the ePals Tour (http://community.epals.com/groups/about/pages/epals-overview.aspx). Have students create individual accounts and practice e-mailing each other.

4. Familiarize students with the National Geographic Map Machine (http://maps.nationalgeographic.com/map-machine.html) and the CIA World Factbook (https://www.cia.gov/library/publications/the-world-factbook).

Lesson One

OBJECTIVES

- Understand that some of our food travels long distances before it becomes available for purchase.

- Understand that the consumer choices we make may impact global warming.

ACTIVITIES

1. Organize the classroom into groups where students can sit down with a computer (ideally, at least one computer for each group of four).

2. In groups, have students review two YouTube videos on the concept of "food miles" and the connection with global warming. The first one is made in England (where half the trucks [lorries] on the highways are carrying food) and refers to the social and environmental impact of our food choices (www.youtube.com/watch?v=tDN9WOeYwDQ). The second one focuses on Australian teenagers who become aware of where their food comes from after visiting the supermarket (www.youtube.com/watch?v=6g8d80LgiXU).

3. Have students discuss their food labels and indicate on the National Geographic Map Machine where the food originates.

4. Have students discuss the positive and negative consequences of increased choices in the supermarket and decide whether the benefits of continuing to transport food over large distances outweigh the risks.

5. After the discussion, have students view a video (www.youtube.com/watch?v=KwtGuXQgPRs) of Dr. Bill Chameides, dean of Duke University's environmental school and lead blogger of www.thegreengrok.com, in which he gives tips on how to fight global warming by retooling trips to the grocery store.

Lesson Two

OBJECTIVES

- Students will learn about cross-cultural communication and the need to observe appropriate "netiquette."

- Students will learn how to adjust style and tone for a culturally different audience.

- Students will use Internet resources to research specific aspects of another country.

ACTIVITIES

1. Have student groups research the country that they will be working with in this lesson. As homework, using the CIA World Factbook (www.cia.gov/library/publications/the-world-factbook/) and other appropriate Internet resources, have students research the country in question (location, population, agriculture, transportation, foods commonly consumed). Each group should come up with two lists: how the country is similar to theirs and how it is different.

2. Have students visit the following "netiquette" website: www.learnthenet.com/english/lessons/150lesson.htm. Lead students in a discussion of appropriate etiquette and sensitivity when communicating with their international partners.

3. Ask students to prepare a group introductory e-mail for their international partners, using ePals, that will report their findings regarding their own typical meal, how many "food miles" their food has traveled, and what recommendations for change they have concerning the issue of global warming and its connection to food production and distribution. In the same e-mail, students should present a series of questions on these same topics to their international counterparts to better understand how these issues impact their partners' country.

Lesson Three

OBJECTIVES

- Students will compare and contrast their own food choices and attitudes with those of the counterpart classroom.

- Using PowerPoint, students will construct a persuasive multimedia presentation for an authentic audience.

- Students will reflect on what they have learned.

ACTIVITIES

1. As homework, student groups will review the answers they received from the counterpart school and compose a report for class discussion concerning similarities and differences between the two countries on the relevant topics. They will draw conclusions about the sources of their own food supply and analyze their own meal in comparison to that of their international counterparts. Student groups will present their findings to the class for discussion.

2. In class, students groups will create a PowerPoint presentation concerning the connection between food choices and global warming and will recommend earth-friendly ways to shop. Students will refer to key concepts such as "food miles," "carbon greenhouse emissions," and "global warming." Later, students will present their work to a PTA or other adult group.

3. As homework, students will write personal reflections on whether they believe their new knowledge might influence their food shopping habits now or in the future. Why or why not?

ASSESSMENTS

- **Group participation** (see http://rubistar.4teachers.org/index.php?&screen=ShowRubric&rubric_id=1638644&).

  Recommended weight: 20 percent

- **Multimedia presentation** for an authentic audience (see http://rubistar.4teachers.org/index.php?screen=ShowRubric&rubric_id=1638671&).

  Recommended weight: 35 percent

- **Self Assessment** (see http://rubistar.4teachers.org/index.php?screen=ShowRubric&rubric_id=1638726&).

  Recommended weight: 10 percent

- **Personal reflection** (see standard rubric: http://rubistar.4teachers.org/index.php?screen=ShowRubric&rubric_id=1638741&).

  Recommended weight: 35 percent

EXTENSIONS

For a background on the Community Food Movement, see Cornell University's Discovering the Food System: A Primer on Community Food Systems: Linking Food, Nutrition and Agriculture: http://foodsys.cce.cornell.edu/primer.html.

For information on the concept of "Food Miles" and facts on how far food in the U.S. travels (1300–2000 miles from farm to consumer), visit the National Sustainable Agriculture Service at: http://attra.ncat.org/farm_energy/food_miles.html.

For insights concerning U.S. activism on this front, see "Think Global, Eat Local" at: www.voiceyourself.com/site/the_big_issues/article.php?article_id=1354/.

For the UK, read about the movement to grow more produce locally based on the costs incurred following the current distribution system in the following: http://news.bbc.co.uk/2/hi/uk_news/4684693.stm http://blogs.guardian.co.uk/food/2007/07/excerpts_from_this_blog_post.html.

Video by Seattle students on advantages of eating healthy local foods: http://bridgesweb.org/project_videos/Seattle/seattle_200708/projSea_localfood.html.

Cross-Cultural Pen Pals

Subjects English/language arts, global education

Grades 6–8

Summary
    Students will communicate via e-mail with students in another country. The purpose is to find out how audience impacts the writing process. Students analyze their own writing and become sensitive to how the audience affects the style, the content, and the purpose of their writing. Students use technology (i.e., e-mail) to make the world a smaller place and to access students of different cultures.

Suggested time allowance three one-hour lessons for preparation, two one-hour lessons for the project, and then time may be reserved to continue work on the project over a six-week period.

RELEVANT STANDARDS

TOPIC: WRITING FORMAT

McREL LANGUAGE ARTS

Standard 1. Uses the general skills and strategies of the writing process

Level III (Grades 6–8)

Benchmark 1. Prewriting: Uses a variety of prewriting strategies (e.g., makes outlines, uses published pieces as writing models, constructs critical standards, brainstorms, builds background knowledge).

Benchmark 2. Drafting and Revising: Uses a variety of strategies to draft and revise written work (e.g., analyzes and clarifies meaning, makes structural and syntactical changes, uses an organizational scheme, uses sensory words and figurative language, rethinks and rewrites for different audiences and purposes, checks for a consistent point of view and for transitions between paragraphs, uses direct feedback to revise compositions).

NATIONAL EDUCATIONAL TECHNOLOGY STANDARDS FOR STUDENTS

2. **Communication and Collaboration**
Students use digital media and environments to communicate and work collaboratively, including at a distance, to support individual learning and contribute to the learning of others.

3. **Research and Information Fluency**
Students apply digital tools to gather, evaluate, and use the information.

5. **Digital Citizenship**
Students understand human, cultural, and societal issues related to technology and practice legal and ethical behavior.

THE AMERICAN FORUM FOR GLOBAL EDUCATION

II. **Culture and World Areas:**

1. Students will know and understand at least one other culture in addition to their own. Students should study at least one culture in-depth and from many different points of view.

2. Students will have a general knowledge about the major geographic and cultural areas of the world and the issues and challenges that unite and divide them. Students should study the major geographical and cultural regions of the world, as well as some of the major issues and challenges that unite and divide these world cultural regions.

RESOURCES

Computers with Internet connection

ePals (www.epals.com) or KidLink (www.kidlink.org/kidspace/index.php) e-mail accounts for students

EduSpaces (http://eduspaces.net) blogging accounts for students

PREPARATION

1. The teacher registers his or her classrooms and interests using KidLink or ePals and connects with another teacher who is interested in a cultural exchange that will involve limited use of class time (students can write their e-mails outside of class time).

2. The teacher spends a class period:
   a. explaining to students the project's goals and the dos and don'ts of appropriate, culturally sensitive correspondence,
   b. introducing students to e-mailing via ePals or KidLink, and
   c. introducing students to blogging via EduSpaces.

3. Students spend two other classroom periods researching the counterpart country or region.

OBJECTIVES

- To understand how to communicate with someone from another culture appropriately.
- To improve students' writing based on their understanding of a real audience.
- To promote a global perspective.

ACTIVITIES

1. Have students answer some or all of the following KidLink questions: www.kidlink.org/english/general/life/belief.html.

2. As homework, students compose a "Who Am I?" personal essay based on their answers to the KidLink questions. In writing the essay, students should keep in mind that an international partner will be their audience.

3. In class, students share their "Who Am I?" essays with a partner for feedback and revision, keeping in mind their ultimate audience.

4. Using their "Who Am I?" personal essay as an introduction, students begin a six-week e-mail correspondence with an international

counterpart. Although this correspondence may range far and wide, students should be reminded often that their ultimate goal is to learn about their penpal and his or her country, and to communicate in ways that reflect appropriate etiquette and cultural sensitivity.

5. Students start a blog chronicling what they already know and what they are learning about their counterpart's country throughout a six-week project. Students post snippets of e-mail exchanges to support their assertions. Students from both countries should be encouraged to read each other's blogs and comment.

ASSESSMENTS

- **Who Am I? essay**
  (www.kidlink.org/kie/nls/english/response/1STQUESTION.html)
  Recommended weight: 60 percent

- **Journal/E-mails:** Students present five chosen blog entries and five e-mail exchanges. (www.kidlink.org/kie/nls/currcon.html)
  Recommended weight: 40 percent

The Mid-continent Research for Education and Learning (McREL) standards can be found in full at www.mcrel.org/compendium/browse.asp.

The ISTE NETS can be found in full at www.iste.org/nets/.

The American Forum on the Humanities standards can be found in full at www.globaled.org/guidelines/index.php.

APPENDIX A
Glossary

Asynchronous Communication   A method of communication that does not rely on the communicators all being available at the same time. For example, e-mail is usually an asynchronous exchange, whereas instant messaging is typically **synchronous**.

Blog   A website hosted by an individual or a group who posts regular entries as a running commentary. In addition to text, other materials, such as graphics, links, and videos, may be included in posts. From the original term "web log."

California Telemation Project   The Telemation project is the name of a California grant-funded training project that in 1994 trained around 400 teachers in information literacy with a focus on how to access and evaluate information from multiple sources.

Cultural Exchange   An exchange visit between citizens of different countries; individuals visit each other's countries of origin to learn about a different culture and its people.

Digital Identities   The collective presence that any individual has online, via mentions in news items, social networking, blogs, and so on. Just as we have a physical identity in the real world—shaped by the way we look, our names, our style of dress—many of us have a web presence as well. "Google" your own name to get an idea of your digital identity.

Digital Immigrants   The term for those of us who did not grow up with digital technologies and are less adept with their use.

Digital Natives   This term was coined by Marc Prensky and refers to the ease with which many young people, by virtue of having grown up with digital technologies, can use and integrate technology.

Digital Story   A story told using multimedia tools such as video, audio, and graphics.

Appendix A • Glossary

File Sharing   Sending and receiving digital files using a network.

FTP   File transfer protocol (FTP) allows program files to be transferred via the Internet between computers.

Global Academy   A school or part of a school's academic program that has a clear and consistent global theme to organize the curriculum. Two converging forces have stimulated the growth of global academies—the first is the rapid growth of schools that have adopted the International Baccalaureate Exam and have organized either their entire curriculum or significant parts of it around the global demands of the exam (the number of schools worldwide who have adopted parts or the entire program is over 13% between 2008 and 2009, www.ibo.org/facts/fastfacts/. The second trend has been the growth of charter and magnet schools that can create specialized programs, such as Colorado's Global Village Academy, www.globalvillageacademy.org/history-of-gva, or the East Hartford Public Schools–Connecticut International Baccalaureate Academy, www.cibanet.org/page.cfm?p=4136.

Global Awareness   A frame of reference that embodies tolerance of cultural differences and knowledge of cultures, history, and global economic, social, and political trends.

Global Education   An approach that fosters cross-cultural awareness, cooperation, and understanding.

Global Educator   An educator who infuses teaching and learning with global perspective.

Global Perspective   The practice of looking at the world through the lens of those who may view events and facts differently because of geographic and cultural differences.

Instant Messaging   A form of synchronous communication between two or more participants utilizing primarily typed text shared via computer connections over a network.

Monocultural   Having the characteristics of a lack of cultural diversity and representing the homogeneous viewpoint of the dominant culture.

Ning   A free social network created by Marc Andreessen and Gina Bianchini in 2004 that enables users to connect around common interests. An account may be accessed through www.ning.com. A classroom ning can be set up through this address along with a wiki.

Podcast   A series of audio (or video) media files distributed via the Internet using RSS feeds. A true podcast is a series of audio or video files made available on a regular basis around a theme. The creator may be referred to as a **podcaster**.

Reflective Blog   Instructional conversations that take place in the blog environment. Resource: Konrad Glogowski, How to Grow a Blog and Towards Reflective Blog Talk, Feb. 4, 2008: www.teachandlearn.ca/blog/2008/02/04/towards-reflective-blogtalk/.

RSS Feeds   An automated way of accessing regularly updated content on the Internet, such as podcasts, blogs, and news items. RSS stands for *real simple syndication*.

Scaffolding   An instructional technique whereby the teacher models the desired learning strategy or task, then gradually shifts responsibility to the students.

Screencast   A screencast is a digitized recording played onscreen, used to show how to use a particular software or computer capability.

Skype   Software that allows users to make free worldwide telephone calls over the Internet using their computers.

Skypecast   A group conference using Skype that allows people to participate by phone via their computers at no cost.

Social Learning   Focuses on how children and adults learn informally from each other through conversation, observation, and modeling behavior.

Social Networking   Virtual communities that exist through sites such as Facebook, MySpace, LinkedIn, and many others.

Story Board   Most commonly a visual sketching out of the plan for a video project that demonstrates plot and events through a sequence of pictures. Storyboarding may also be used to plan a piece of writing or an audio project.

Synchronous Communication   A method of communication that depends on all communicators being available at the same time (real time). For example, a telephone conversation or an instant messaging conversation is typically synchronous, while e-mail is typically **asynchronous**.

Videoconference   Interactive telecommunications technologies that allow two or more locations to interact via two-way video and audio simultaneously.

Virtual Meeting   A meeting where all participants need not be present in the same location. Technologies such as videoconferencing, instant messaging, conference calling, and Skype make virtual meetings possible.

Appendix A • **Glossary**

Virtual Reality   A high-end user interface that involves real-time 3D simulations and interactions via multimedia information. Second Life, Teen Second Life, and Lively are examples.

Voice over Internet Protocol (VoIP)   Delivery of voice communications over the Internet.

VoiceThread   According to the VoiceThread website, "VoiceThread is an online media album that can hold essentially any type of media (images, documents and videos) and allows people to make comments in 5 different ways—using voice (with a microphone or telephone), text, audio file, or video (with a webcam)—and share them with anyone they wish. They can even be exported to an Archival Movie for offline use on a DVD or video-enabled MP3 player. A VoiceThread allows group conversations to be collected and shared in one place, from anywhere in the world." (http://voicethread.com/about/).

Vlog   A blog that is video-based instead of text-based.

Vodcast   A video-based podcast rather than an audio-based podcast.

Web 2.0   An Internet movement wherein websites have tended to move away from being static repositories of information updated only by the website owner, to being highly interactive tools that visitors can use to share, tag, and comment on digital files of all kinds; to publish themselves in text, audio, or video forms; and to connect with others via social networking.

Webinar   A one-way seminar broadcast over the Internet with limited audience interaction.

WebQuest   An inquiry-based activity supported by the Internet and often supplemented with videoconferencing. There are usually a list of Internet links to follow to complete the activity, like an online slide show.

Widget   A piece of software that can be inserted easily into a webpage and often provides updateable or interactive information such as the time, a map, a newsfeed, or an alert.

Wiki   A collection of interlinked webpages enabling participants to add and edit content using simplified markup language. *Wikipedia* (www.wikipedia.org) is the most well-known example of a wiki.

Windows Movie Maker   A video-creating/editing software included in Microsoft Windows. It contains features such as effects, transitions, titles/credits, audio track, timeline narration, and *Auto Movie*. New effects and transitions can be made and existing ones can be modified using XML (Extensible Markup Language) code.

APPENDIX B
Web Resources

There are hundreds of wonderful Internet resources available for the savvy global educator. Quite a few are mentioned in the main text; here are even more!

For Competitive Students

If you want to motivate your students and challenge them at the same time, the best starting point is finding the right contest. Here are a few opportunities.

U.S. State Department's "Doors to Diplomacy"
www.globalschoolnet.org/gsndoors/index.cfm

The U.S. State Department's "Doors to Diplomacy" is a good place for students to try their hands at examining world issues and using the web to communicate their opinions. Student teams consist of two to four students between the ages of 12 and 19 years. The annual competition asks students to prepare a website that educates other students about a subject related to a published category, such as Peace and Democracy. Each member of the winning Doors to Diplomacy Award team receives a $2,000 scholarship. The winning coaches' schools each receive a $500 cash award, and each winning team member and coach receives a special plaque from the U.S. State Department.

ThinkQuest Competition
http://thinkquest.org

The ThinkQuest Competition sets the challenge for students working in teams to create the best educational website. One prize is given to the website that represents the best global perspective and appeals to a diverse audience with content "addressing an important issue facing humanity." The competition is divided into three age divisions: 12 and under, 15 and under, and 19 and under. Winners receive laptops or other computer hardware.

For Younger Students

Flat Stanley
www.flatstanley.com/curriculum.htm

The Flat Stanley project started with a book, *Flat Stanley*, by Jeff Brown and Scott Nash. The book's unusual premise is that Stanley, an otherwise normal boy, is squashed flat by a falling bulletin board. Since he is flat, he can be folded into an envelope and travel great distances quite cheaply. Students create paper Flat Stanleys and start a journal detailing their lives with him, and then the character and the journal are sent to another school, and the process repeats itself. Students can plot their travels on maps and share the contents of the journal. Often, a Flat Stanley returns with a pin or postcard from his visit. Some teachers prefer to use e-mail only, and this is noted in the list of participants on the Flat Stanley project site. Some curriculum applications, such as calculating how far Flat Stanley traveled for mathematics, are included on the website.

ThinkQuest
www.thinkquest.org/en/projects/index.html

ThinkQuest (formerly Think.com) "is a protected, online learning platform that enables teachers to integrate learning projects into their classroom curriculum and students to develop 21st century skills." It allows students to communicate with students in other countries using secure e-mail. The site has many simple and well-designed modules that allow students to get started working collaboratively to create secure (non-public) web-based projects. The site contains several beginner projects for Grades 5 through 8, such as asking students to describe their community to someone from another country.

KidProj
www.kidlink.org/KIDPROJ

KidProj is run by 500 volunteers in more than 50 countries and was created by two Norwegians, one American, and a Canadian. Hundreds of public and private virtual "rooms" are used for discussion and collaboration. Information is available in more than 30 languages from Kidlink. Students through secondary schools join global projects. Teachers and youth group leaders from around the world plan activities and projects for their students in the adult discussion area. Student work is posted on the web in Kidlink's KidSpace. One of the more accessible projects on the Kidlink site for elementary school students is "Grandmother and Me," where students from around the world describe how they feel about their grandmothers, what they call her, and how she is special to them. The students can also write collaborative stories about their grandmothers and generally use their art and creativity to express ideas and bridge language barriers.

For Student Environmentalists

GlobalEd
www.globaleducation.edna.edu.au/globaled/page1.html

GlobalEd is a project of Australia's Agency for International Development (AusAID). It produces a number of case studies to be used in teaching about various environmental issues in various countries of the world.

Baltic Sea Project
www.bspinfo.lt

The Baltic Sea Project of UNESCO's Associated Schools Project has students in schools of several nations surrounding the Baltic Sea working on both environmental and intercultural issues.

Center for Global Involvement Education
www.hamline.edu/education/cgee_site

The Center for Global Involvement Education at Hamline University in St. Paul, Minnesota, provides teacher in-service programs and online curricula that "engage students in hands-on learning and environmental stewardship."

Appendix B • Web Resources

Mega Sites Offering a Range of Resources and Lesson Plans

Oxfam
www.oxfam.org.uk/education

The Oxfam site contains hundreds of online materials, lesson plans, and resources for globally-aware lessons. It is a very easy site to navigate, organized by grade level, topics, and areas of study.

National Geographic's Xpeditions
www.nationalgeographic.com/xpeditions

If you teach geography or social studies, it is hard not to be impressed by the National Geographic's Xpeditions website, built around the National Geography Standards—presenting teachers with lesson plans and activities including a variety of missions for students to undertake in a video-game-like environment called Xpedition Hall.

Globe
http://globe.gov

Globe is a worldwide community of students, teachers, scientists, and citizens "working together to better understand, sustain, and improve Earth's environment at local, regional, and global scales." Students plan projects to collect data and research using some common topics and guidelines in collaboration with partners throughout the world.

Coverdell World Wise Schools
www.peacecorps.gov/wws

The Coverdell World Wise Schools program of the Peace Corps organizes lesson plans by grade level, region, and by subject area—many of them containing video material and a generous sprinkling of Peace Corps quotes and insights. From this site you also can sign up to receive an e-newsletter, *World Wise Window*, with current educational information on Peace Corps volunteers' projects.

Teacher's Guide to International Collaboration
www.ed.gov/teachers/how/tech/international/index.html

The U.S. Department of Education published its Teacher's Guide to International Collaboration shortly after 9/11 as part of the Department of Education's International

Education Initiative. It was developed "to help teachers use the Internet to reach out globally."

Global Education Motivators
www.globalgateway.org.uk

Global Education Motivators has a special interest in disseminating the work of the United Nations. Among its activities to support the UN, it runs a series of videoconferences that "connect students with each other to explore the work of the UN."

School Partnering Services

Global Gateway
www.globalgateway.org.uk/default.aspx?page=325

Global Gateway offers an easy way to find schools to partner with to collaborate on projects or just to communicate about common interests. The interface is simple and requires you to send a message to a school that has expressed an interest in partnering by responding to some simple questions such as: Are you keen to plan work each week, each month? Do you have clear learning goals? Can the students work together?

Global Learning Communities
www.glc.me.uk

The Global Learning Communities concept was born in 2003 when a pilot group of some 70 Bedfordshire, UK, schools (all ages of students) received UK government funding to develop shared learning links around the time zones of the world. The concept is that schools might begin to give their students a grasp of the new global realities where work is collaborative across countries and can continue across time zones 24/7. To reflect these realities, the site offers students an online newspaper to contribute to (www.glc.me.uk/247news). Global Learning Communities also sponsors an online conference area where students can discuss contemporary issues with a global perspective. A forum provides a simulation college with a theater-like discussion area containing multimedia presentations on an aspect of the topic, a place for informal conversations, a conference area for guided discussions, and an exhibition hall for projects.

Associated Schools Project Network
www.unesco.org/education/asp

The Associated Schools Project Network is coordinated by several international organizations, including UNESCO. Network schools become part of ASPNet and "are encouraged to conduct pilot projects on four main themes of study covering a wide range of interrelated subtopics. The point of departure should be issues relevant to the student's own environment, concerns, and aspirations." The themes include poverty, disease, unemployment, human rights, democracy, and tolerance. Schools often choose the Universal Declaration of Human Rights, the Convention on the Rights of the Child, or the Decade on Education for Human Rights (1995–2004), for example, as points of departure.

SchoolNet Africa
www.schoolnetafrica.org

SchoolNet Africa projects are in about 30 African countries and demonstrate growing interest from governments, schools, and the private sector. The demand for SchoolNet Africa has evolved from national school networking programs. One of the website sections, Learner Center, provides space for international online collaboration among young people.

Excellent Lesson Plan Resources

Amnesty International
www.amnestyusa.org/educate/lesson-plans/page.do?id=1102163

The Amnesty International site includes lesson plans and teacher guides on a large range of human rights issues affecting countries around the world.

CNN Students News
www.cnn.com/studentnews

CNN Students News is geared toward K–12 learners, can provide students with a true sense of global stories, and includes useful quizzes and classroom exercises.

Cyber UN Schoolbus
www.un.org/Pubs/CyberSchoolBus/cur.html

Cyber UN Schoolbus has many curriculum units available on this website, among them, the dangers of landmines, racial discrimination, peace education, cleaner oceans, women's rights, and human rights—all with an emphasis on the role the UN plays related to these issues.

Global Climate Change
www.climatechangeeducation.org/k-12/index.html

Global Climate Change is a comprehensive site developed by docents and volunteers at California science centers and museums and by students, scientists, and staff at the University of California, Berkeley. Interdisciplinary lesson plans focus on the use of Internet resources to promote hands-on science demonstrations and provide materials related to math, language arts, writing, careers, history, and more.

Newseum
www.newseum.org/todaysfrontpages/default.asp

Newseum contains up to 80 newspaper front pages from 48 countries. The site can be made far more valuable if students are assigned the task of composing a set of world newspaper headlines from a review of 10–20 international newspapers. Or, ask students to compare the ways a particular event is covered by different countries' newspapers.

New York Times
www.nytimes.com/learning/teachers/lessons/globalhistory.html

The *New York Times* offers an extensive library of lesson plans (using a searchable database) that have a news focus and are constantly being updated.

Oxfam
www.oxfam.org.uk/education/resources/category.htm?9

This British organization's site includes a number of lesson plans targeted for middle school grades that include informative and enjoyable activities exploring everything from improvising traditions of different cultures and styles, to how music is used to convey social, political, and cultural messages. "Oxfam works in education policy and practice to empower young people to be active Global Citizens. We promote education

Appendix B • Web Resources

that helps young people understand the global issues that affect their lives and take action towards a more just and sustainable world." See also *Education for Global Citizenship: A Guide for Schools* at www.oxfam.org.uk/education/gc/files/education_for_global_citizenship_a_guide_for_schools.pdf.

PBS The WIDE ANGLE Global Classroom
www.pbs.org/wnet/wideangle/classroom/index.html

The Public Broadcasting Service (PBS) offers lesson plans and activities for middle school and high school teachers. Most WIDE ANGLE episodes may be purchased for educational and non-theatrical use. The topics range from "Gang Violence from L.A. to El Salvador" (what is being done to stem the influence of gangs that have spread from Central America) to "Accountability for Human Rights Violations" to "Divided Peninsula: Six Decades of Military and Political Tension in Korea." The lesson on Korea provides a framework for discussion of Korea to help students understand the history of this divided nation and to become more knowledgeable in their analysis of current news issues.

PBS Now Program
www.pbs.org/now/classroom/globalwarming.html

The PBS Now Program has lesson plans concerning global warming based on their video documentaries.

Peace Corps
www.csun.edu/~hcedu013/plans.html#Lesson%20Plans
www.peacecorps.gov/wws/educators

Peace Corps developed lessons for students in Grades 3–12 to help teachers integrate global education into daily lessons. Additionally, World Wise Schools has "helped more than 3 million U.S. students communicate directly with Peace Corps volunteers all over the world. Initially set up as a correspondence match program between volunteers and U.S. classes, World Wise Schools expanded its scope over almost two decades by providing a broad range of resources for educators." Even if you choose not to communicate with a Peace Corps volunteer, the site is still valuable because of the lesson plans, videos, and primary source materials.

Also Recommended

Telecollaborate!
http://nschubert.home.mchsi.com

The Telecollaborate! website provides the tools for teachers to design, develop, and publish their telecollaborative projects.

International Baccalaureate Organisation (IBO)
www.ibo.org

The International Baccalaureate Organisation (IBO) is a nonprofit education foundation based in Switzerland that offers an academic diploma program for students in the final two years of secondary school and a middle school program for younger students. It has grown to more than 450 participating schools in over 60 countries.

Phi Delta Kappan Resource Guide
www.pdkintl.org/kappan/k_v86/k0411ka3.htm

The Phi Delta Kappan Resource Guide provides a variety of resources for international education, including classroom materials, professional development opportunities for educators, and international programs for students.

Asia Society
www.asiasociety.org

The Asia Society promotes dialogue concerning global issues with particular attention to Asian-American relations.

American Forum for Global Education
www.globaled.org

The American Forum for Global Education is a private nonprofit organization that provides diverse resources designed to provide leadership and assistance for school systems, state departments of education, and colleges and universities. The site is undergoing transition at the moment to include a number of new resources, including an index of project topics, lesson plans, and assignments.

Center for Teaching International Relations (CTIR)
www.du.edu/ctir

The Center for Teaching International Relations (CTIR) is the outreach arm of the University of Denver Graduate School of International Studies. CTIR's 40-year history of helping K–12 educators teach about global affairs is reflected in its wide range of programs (World Affairs Challenge, Rocky Mountain Model United Nations) and publications (*Area Studies*, *Global Issues*, *Cultural Studies*, *Economics & Environment*, *Reading & Writing*, *Art*), all promoting international education and understanding in K–12 classrooms.

Choices Education Program
www.watsoninstitute.org/program_detail.cfm?id=1

The Choices Education Program provides a whole library of high school materials for teachers, both historical and topical, drawing on the expertise of Brown University's Watson Institute for International Studies. The materials are designed to promote critical thinking and use multiple perspectives and competing interpretations.

Earth Force
www.earthforce.org

The Earth Force site is ideal for those elementary, middle, and high school teachers who believe that a focus on environmental education should also be an opportunity to encourage critical thinking. Among the most popular programs is the Global Rivers Environmental Education Network (GREEN), which focuses on providing middle and high school students with opportunities to "acquire essential academic skills including critical thinking, teamwork, problem solving and decision making, all while actively engaging in their communities around water quality issues. To do so, educators use an award-winning curriculum, Protecting Our Watersheds, and rely on the support of GREEN staff to correlate these experiences to required learning standards."

Global Learning and Observations to Benefit the Environment (GLOBE)
www.globe.gov

The Global Learning and Observations to Benefit the Environment (GLOBE) project consists of a partnership among schools, colleges, universities, the National Oceanic and Atmospheric Administration (NOAA), the National Aeronautics and Space Administration (NASA), the National Science Foundation (NSF), the Environmental Protection Agency (EPA), and 95 other countries. "GLOBE provides students with a more integrated view of the various subjects they study and supports curricula interconnections in all areas. Interdisciplinary GLOBE projects have included science, mathematics, technology, geography, social studies, language, culture, art, music, physical education, cross-age collaborations, service learning projects, life-long learning opportunities and community involvement."

Kidlink
www.kidlink.org

Kidlink, a nonprofit organization based in Sweden, provides an easy way to introduce global issues to elementary school students through projects that find commonalities among students around the world—the "Who Am I?" and "Grandmother and Me" projects are models of their kind. The site is available in more than 20 different languages.

Model United Nations Headquarters
http://cyberschoolbus.un.org/modelun/index.asp

The Model United Nations Headquarters site provides comprehensive information about the UN and its activities in a highly accessible form. Start with the Overview and the FAQs, and you will begin to gain a sense of the multiple ways the site can be used. Participation in the interactive forums is sponsored by iEARN.

And Many, Many More!

Amnesty International USA—Human Rights Education: **www.amnestyusa.org/educate/about/page.do?id=1102103&n1=4&n2=79&n3=1340/** and Lesson plans and resources: **www.amnesty.org.au/hre/comments/2310/**. Also from AI: Curriculum Guides: **www.amnestyusa.org/film-curriculum-guides/blood-diamond-curriculum-guide/pagedo?id=1102105&n1=4&n2=79&n3=1509/**.

Animal Diaries from TESAN: The Endangered Species and Nature of the World: **www.tesan.vuurwerk.nl/diaries/**. This project was designed by Joan Goble and Rene de Vries and their students (see Chapter 2, this volume). The site is useful as an example of a project soliciting input from children around the world.

Animoto (for educators): **http://education.animoto.com**
(geared for students): **http://animoto.com**

Babelfish (text and webpage translation): **http://babelfish.yahoo.com**

Blogger: **www.blogger.com**

Appendix B • Web Resources

California Arts Project, The (TCAP) (TCAP is the sponsor of the California Telemation Project.): **http://csmp.ucop.edu/tcap/resources/telemation_project.html**

CIA World Factbook: **www.cia.gov/library/publications/the-world-factbook**

City Quest: **www.cityquest.nl**

CountryWatch: **www.countrywatch.com**

Digital Storyteller: **www.digitalstoryteller.com**

Discovery Education: **http://school.discoveryeducation.com**

ePals: **www.epals.com**

ePals School Blog: **www.epals.com/products/esb**

Eduspaces: **http://eduspaces.net**

European Schoolnet: **www.eun.org/portal/index.htm**

Evoca: **www.evoca.com**

Facebook: **www.facebook.com**

Feeding Minds Fighting Hunger: **www.feedingminds.org**

Flat Classroom Project: **http://flatclassroomproject.wikispaces.com**

Flickr: **www.flickr.com**

Friends and Flags: **www.friendsandflags.org**

Global Kids: **www.globalkids.org**

Global Kidz: **www.gigglepotz.com/globalkidz1.htm**

Global Nomads: **www.gng.org**

Global Schoolhouse and Global SchoolNet: **www.globalschoolnet.org**

Global Youth Voices: **www.globalyouthvoices.org**

Google Earth: **http://earth.google.com**

Google Groups: **http://groups.google.com**

Google News: **http://news.google.com**

Horizon Project: **http://horizonproject.wikispaces.com/Resources**

iEARN: www.iearn.org

Jason Project: www.jason.org

Kidlink: www.kidlink.org/kidspace/index.php

Mathlincs: The Global Education Collaborative: http://globaleducation.ning.com/forum/topic/show?id=717180%3ATopic%3A17625

My Hero: www.myhero.com/myhero

MySpace: www.myspace.com

NASA Education: http://education.nasa.gov/divisions/eleandsec/overview/index.html

National Geographic's Map Machine: http://maps.nationalgeographic.com/mapmachine

National Public Radio (NPR): www.npr.org

Newseum: www.newseum.org and www.newseum.org/todaysfrontpages/default.asp

NOAA (National Oceanic & Atmospheric Administration) Education: www.education.noaa.gov

1001 Flat World Tales: http://es1001tales2009.wikispaces.com

One True Media: www.onetruemedia.com

Oxfam: www.oxfam.org.uk/education/resources/ and www.oxfam.org.uk/education/resources/global_music_lesson_plans

Passport to Antartica: http://passporttoknowledge.com/antarctica

Passport to Knowledge: http://passporttoknowledge.com/main.html

Rubistar: http://rubistar.4teachers.org/index.php

Science Across the World: www.scienceacross.org

ScrapBlog: www.scrapblog.com

Screencast-O-Matic: www.screencast-o-matic.com/watch/cijnoqvu

Second Life: http://secondlife.com
(adults only)

Skype: www.skype.com

Survey Monkey: www.surveymonkey.com

Taking IT Global: www.tigweb.org

Teen Second Life: http://teen.secondlife.com

30Boxes: www.30boxes.com

Travel Buddies: www.globalschoolnet.org/programs/travelbuddies

UNICEF (United Nations Children's Fund) Lifeskills: www.unicef.org/lifeskills/index_whichskills.html

UNICEF Voices of Youth: www.unicef.org/voy

VoiceThread: http://voicethread.com/#home

Wikispaces: www.wikispaces.com
and www.wikispaces.com/site/for/teachers

Windows Movie Maker 2.1 Download: www.microsoft.com/windowsxp/downloads/updates/moviemaker2.mspx

Worldbank You Think Issues: http://youthink.worldbank.org/issues/education/

Youth Voices: http://youthvoices.net

YouTube: www.youtube.com

APPENDIX C

National Educational Technology Standards

National Educational Technology Standards for Students (NETS•S)

All K–12 students should be prepared to meet the following standards and performance indicators.

1. **Creativity and Innovation**

    Students demonstrate creative thinking, construct knowledge, and develop innovative products and processes using technology. Students:

    a. apply existing knowledge to generate new ideas, products, or processes

    b. create original works as a means of personal or group expression

    c. use models and simulations to explore complex systems and issues

    d. identify trends and forecast possibilities

Appendix C • National Educational Technology Standards

2. **Communication and Collaboration**

   Students use digital media and environments to communicate and work collaboratively, including at a distance, to support individual learning and contribute to the learning of others. Students:

   a. interact, collaborate, and publish with peers, experts, or others employing a variety of digital environments and media

   b. communicate information and ideas effectively to multiple audiences using a variety of media and formats

   c. develop cultural understanding and global awareness by engaging with learners of other cultures

   d. contribute to project teams to produce original works or solve problems

3. **Research and Information Fluency**

   Students apply digital tools to gather, evaluate, and use information. Students:

   a. plan strategies to guide inquiry

   b. locate, organize, analyze, evaluate, synthesize, and ethically use information from a variety of sources and media

   c. evaluate and select information sources and digital tools based on the appropriateness to specific tasks

   d. process data and report results

4. **Critical Thinking, Problem Solving, and Decision Making**

   Students use critical-thinking skills to plan and conduct research, manage projects, solve problems, and make informed decisions using appropriate digital tools and resources. Students:

   a. identify and define authentic problems and significant questions for investigation

b. plan and manage activities to develop a solution or complete a project

c. collect and analyze data to identify solutions and make informed decisions

d. use multiple processes and diverse perspectives to explore alternative solutions

5. **Digital Citizenship**

    Students understand human, cultural, and societal issues related to technology and practice legal and ethical behavior. Students:

    a. advocate and practice the safe, legal, and responsible use of information and technology

    b. exhibit a positive attitude toward using technology that supports collaboration, learning, and productivity

    c. demonstrate personal responsibility for lifelong learning

    d. exhibit leadership for digital citizenship

6. **Technology Operations and Concepts**

    Students demonstrate a sound understanding of technology concepts, systems, and operations. Students:

    a. understand and use technology systems

    b. select and use applications effectively and productively

    c. troubleshoot systems and applications

    d. transfer current knowledge to the learning of new technologies

National Educational Technology Standards for Teachers (NETS·T)

All classroom teachers should be prepared to meet the following standards and performance indicators.

1. **Facilitate and Inspire Student Learning and Creativity**

    Teachers use their knowledge of subject matter, teaching and learning, and technology to facilitate experiences that advance student learning, creativity, and innovation in both face-to-face and virtual environments. Teachers:

    a. promote, support, and model creative and innovative thinking and inventiveness

    b. engage students in exploring real-world issues and solving authentic problems using digital tools and resources

    c. promote student reflection using collaborative tools to reveal and clarify students' conceptual understanding and thinking, planning, and creative processes

    d. model collaborative knowledge construction by engaging in learning with students, colleagues, and others in face-to-face and virtual environments

2. **Design and Develop Digital-Age Learning Experiences and Assessments**

    Teachers design, develop, and evaluate authentic learning experiences and assessments incorporating contemporary tools and resources to maximize content learning in context and to develop the knowledge, skills, and attitudes identified in the NETS·S. Teachers:

    a. design or adapt relevant learning experiences that incorporate digital tools and resources to promote student learning and creativity

    b. develop technology-enriched learning environments that enable all students to pursue their individual curiosities and become active participants in setting their own educational goals, managing their own learning, and assessing their own progress

c. customize and personalize learning activities to address students' diverse learning styles, working strategies, and abilities using digital tools and resources

d. provide students with multiple and varied formative and summative assessments aligned with content and technology standards and use resulting data to inform learning and teaching

3. **Model Digital-Age Work and Learning**

   Teachers exhibit knowledge, skills, and work processes representative of an innovative professional in a global and digital society. Teachers:

   a. demonstrate fluency in technology systems and the transfer of current knowledge to new technologies and situations

   b. collaborate with students, peers, parents, and community members using digital tools and resources to support student success and innovation

   c. communicate relevant information and ideas effectively to students, parents, and peers using a variety of digital-age media and formats

   d. model and facilitate effective use of current and emerging digital tools to locate, analyze, evaluate, and use information resources to support research and learning

4. **Promote and Model Digital Citizenship and Responsibility**

   Teachers understand local and global societal issues and responsibilities in an evolving digital culture and exhibit legal and ethical behavior in their professional practices. Teachers:

   a. advocate, model, and teach safe, legal, and ethical use of digital information and technology, including respect for copyright, intellectual property, and the appropriate documentation of sources

b. address the diverse needs of all learners by using learner-centered strategies and providing equitable access to appropriate digital tools and resources

c. promote and model digital etiquette and responsible social interactions related to the use of technology and information

d. develop and model cultural understanding and global awareness by engaging with colleagues and students of other cultures using digital-age communication and collaboration tools

5. **Engage in Professional Growth and Leadership**

Teachers continuously improve their professional practice, model lifelong learning, and exhibit leadership in their school and professional community by promoting and demonstrating the effective use of digital tools and resources. Teachers:

a. participate in local and global learning communities to explore creative applications of technology to improve student learning

b. exhibit leadership by demonstrating a vision of technology infusion, participating in shared decision making and community building, and developing the leadership and technology skills of others

c. evaluate and reflect on current research and professional practice on a regular basis to make effective use of existing and emerging digital tools and resources in support of student learning

d. contribute to the effectiveness, vitality, and self-renewal of the teaching profession and of their school and community

National Educational Technology Standards for Administrators (NETS•A)

All school administrators should be prepared to meet the following standards and performance indicators.

1. **Visionary Leadership**

    Educational Administrators inspire and lead development and implementation of a shared vision for comprehensive integration of technology to promote excellence and support transformation throughout the organization. Educational Administrators:

    a. inspire and facilitate among all stakeholders a shared vision of purposeful change that maximizes use of digital-age resources to meet and exceed learning goals, support effective instructional practice, and maximize performance of district and school leaders

    b. engage in an ongoing process to develop, implement, and communicate technology-infused strategic plans aligned with a shared vision

    c. advocate on local, state, and national levels for policies, programs, and funding to support implementation of a technology- infused vision and strategic plan

2. **Digital-Age Learning Culture**

    Educational Administrators create, promote, and sustain a dynamic, digital-age learning culture that provides a rigorous, relevant, and engaging education for all students. Educational Administrators:

    a. ensure instructional innovation focused on continuous improvement of digital-age learning

    b. model and promote the frequent and effective use of technology for learning

c. provide learner-centered environments equipped with technology and learning resources to meet the individual, diverse needs of all learners

d. ensure effective practice in the study of technology and its infusion across the curriculum

e. promote and participate in local, national, and global learning communities that stimulate innovation, creativity, and digital-age collaboration

3. **Excellence in Professional Practice**

Educational Administrators promote an environment of professional learning and innovation that empowers educators to enhance student learning through the infusion of contemporary technologies and digital resources. Educational Administrators:

a. allocate time, resources, and access to ensure ongoing professional growth in technology fluency and integration

b. facilitate and participate in learning communities that stimulate, nurture, and support administrators, faculty, and staff in the study and use of technology

c. promote and model effective communication and collaboration among stakeholders using digital-age tools

d. stay abreast of educational research and emerging trends regarding effective use of technology and encourage evaluation of new technologies for their potential to improve student learning

4. **Systemic Improvement**

Educational Administrators provide digital-age leadership and management to continuously improve the organization through the effective use of information and technology resources. Educational Administrators:

a. lead purposeful change to maximize the achievement of learning goals through the appropriate use of technology and media-rich resources

    b. collaborate to establish metrics, collect and analyze data, interpret results, and share findings to improve staff performance and student learning

    c. recruit and retain highly competent personnel who use technology creatively and proficiently to advance academic and operational goals

    d. establish and leverage strategic partnerships to support systemic improvement

    e. establish and maintain a robust infrastructure for technology including integrated, interoperable technology systems to support management, operations, teaching, and learning

5. **Digital Citizenship**

    Educational Administrators model and facilitate understanding of social, ethical, and legal issues and responsibilities related to an evolving digital culture. Educational Administrators:

        a. ensure equitable access to appropriate digital tools and resources to meet the needs of all learners

        b. promote, model, and establish policies for safe, legal, and ethical use of digital information and technology

        c. promote and model responsible social interactions related to the use of technology and information

        d. model and facilitate the development of a shared cultural understanding and involvement in global issues through the use of contemporary communication and collaboration tools

APPENDIX D

References

Ahmed, A. (2007). *Journey into Islam: The crisis of globalization.* Washington, DC: The Brookings Institution.

Barker, C. M. (2000). Education for international understanding and global competence: Report of a meeting convened by Carnegie Corporation of New York, January 21, 2000. Retrieved from www.carnegie.org/pdf/global.pdf

Bennett, M. (2001, June). Symposium conducted at the Global Partners Project—Best Practices Conference, quoted in final plenary session by Sue Mennicke.

Bishop, B. (2008). *The big sort: Why the clustering of Americans is tearing us apart.* Boston: Houghton Mifflin.

Brown, J. S., & Adler, R. (2008). *Minds on fire: Open education, the long tail, and learning 2.0.* (Educause Jan/Feb 2008). Retrieved August 26, 2008, from http://net.educause.edu/ir/library/pdf/ERM0811.pdf

Burrell, C. (2008). Beyond school (blog). Retrieved August 26, 2008, from http://beyond-school.org/2008/07/25/flat-too-flat-for-teens

Bush, A., Chung, S., Holton, W., & Kokozos, M. (Capstone Team), & Spiro, J. (Capstone advisor). (April 2007). "The New York State–Moscow schools telecommunications project: The founding project of iEarn." New York University, Robert F. Wagner Graduate School of Public Service. Retrieved from www.iearn.org/iEARN_NY-Moscow_Evaluation.pdf

Carvin, A. Video correspondence. May 21, 2007.

Cofino, K. Personal correspondence. September 2008.

Collins, T., Czarra, F. R., & Smith, A. F. (2003). The American Forum for Global Education website. Retrieved April 29, 2009, from www.globaled.org/guidelines/index.php

Comenius, J. [ca. 1649] (1997). *Johann Comenius: The labyrinth of the world and the paradise of the heart.* Translated from Czech and introduced by Howard Louthan and Andrea Sterk. (Classics of Western Spirituality) Mahwah, NJ: Paulist Press.

Copen, P. (2002). International Education and Resource Network (iEARN) Program Evaluation, Evaluation report: Impact on teachers and students who attended the 9th Annual International iEARN Conference in Moscow, Russia 2002. Retrieved August 26, 2008, from www.iearn.org/surveyreport.pdf

Council of Chief State School Officers. (2006). Global education policy statement. Retrieved from www.ccsso.org/content/pdfs/Global Education FINAL lowrez.pdf

Cubberley, E. P. (1909). Changing Conceptions of Education in America. Boston: Houghton, Mifflin.

Cummins, J., Devillar, R. A., & Faltins, C. (1994). *Cultural diversity in schools.* Albany, NY: SUNY Press.

Cummins, J., & Sayers, D. (1995). *Brave new schools: Challenging cultural illiteracy through global learning networks.* New York: Macmillan.

Davis, V. A. (2008). Cool cat teacher (blog). Retrieved August 26, 2008, from http://coolcatteacher.blogspot.com/2008/01/it-is-about-educational-networking-not.html

Davis, V. A., & Lindsay, J. Flat Classroom Project http://flatclassroomproject.wikispaces.com

Davis, V., and Lindsay, J. (2007). Rubric Assessment. Flat Classroom Project 2007. Retrieved July 8, 2009, from http://flatclassroomproject.wikispaces.com/Rubrics

DeVillar, R., & Faltis, C. (1991). *Computers and cultural diversity.* Albany, NY: SUNY Press.

Dewey, J. (1902). The school as social center. In J. A. Boydston (Ed.) (1976), *John Dewey: The middle works, 1899–1924*, Vol. 2: 1902–1903. Carbondale, IL: Southern Illinois University Press.

Downes, S. (n.d.). E-learning 2.0. Retrieved July 8, 2009 from the National Research Council of Canada, http://elearnmag.org/subpage.cfm?section=articles&article=29-1

Downes, S. (2007). *Learning networks in practice*, Vol. 2. Covetry, UK: British Educational Communications and Technology Agency (Becta). Retrieved August 25, 2008, from http://partners.becta.org.uk/upload-dir/downloads/page_documents/research/emerging_technologies07_chapter2.pdf

Engler, J., & Hunt, Jr., J. B. (2004). Preparing our students for work and citizenship in the global age. *Phi Delta Kappan, 86*(3).

Erasmus, D. (1509). *The praise of folly.* Translated by John Wilson (1668). (The Project Gutenberg EBook of The Praise of Folly, by Desiderius Erasmus, 2005, produced by Robert Shimmin and PG Distributed Proofreaders). Retrieved from www.gutenberg.org/dirs/etext05/8efly10.txt

Fiske, S. T. (2000). Interdependence reduces prejudice and stereotyping. In S. Oskamp (Ed.), *Reducing prejudice and discrimination* (pp. 115–135). Mahwah, NJ: Erlbaum.

Flat Classroom Project 2007, Rubric Assessment, http://flatclassroomproject.wikispaces.com/Rubrics

Florida Virtual School. (2006). Florida virtual school students win international diplomacy competition. Retrieved August 26, 2008, from www.ictliteracy.info/rf.pdf/Doors_to_Diplomacy.2006.htm

Friedman, T. (2005). *The world is flat.* NY: Farrar, Straus and Giroux.

Fueling the future. (2006). In *facing the future: People and the planet,* Lesson 17. Retrieved August 25, 2008, from http://facingthefuture.org/Portals/0/documents/GSRLibrary/17.Fueling.Future.pdf

Galinsky, A. D., & Moskowitz, G. B. (2000). Perspective-taking: Decreasing stereotype expression, stereotype accessibility, and in-group favoritism. *Journal of Personality and Social Psychology, 78,* 708–724.

Gartner. (2007). Gartner Says 80 Percent of Active Internet Users Will Have a "Second Life" in the Virtual World by the End of 2011. Retrieved July 8, 2009 from Garnter, www.gartner.com/it/page.jsp?id=503861

Global Kids' digital media initiative. (2004). Retrieved 2004 from www.holymeatballs.org/2007/03/March24

Global Kids' digital media initiative. (2007). Retrieved August 26, 2008, from www.holymeatballs.org/2007/03/teen_panel_talking_about_gk_pr.html

Global Teacher. (n.d.). Web 3.0 community and research project. Retrieved August 26, 2008, from http://globalteacher.org.au/about-global-student

Goble, J. (2004). A world of wonder—My Japan experience. Retrieved August 29, 2008, from www.siec.k12.in.us/cannelton/fmfjapan

Goren, M. www.globaldreamers.org, Petach Tikva, Israel.

Gutek, G. L. (1993). *American education in a global society: Internationalizing teacher education.* Prospect Heights, IL: Waveland Press, Inc.

Hanvey, R. (1976). An attainable global perspective. New York: The American Forum for Global Education. Retrieved August 25, 2008, from www.globaled.org/An_Att_Glob_Persp_04_11_29.pdf

Hicks, D. (2003). Thirty years of global education: A reminder of key principles and precedents. *Educational Review, 55*(3), 265–275.

Hierocles. (2nd century CE). Quoted in M. Nussbaum. (1994). Patriotism and cosmopolitanism. *The Boston Review, 19*(5). Retrieved from www.bsos.umd.edu/gvpt/Theory/Patriotism and Cosmopolitanism.pdf

Hoopes, D. S. (1981). Intercultural communication concepts and the psychology of intercultural experience. In M. D. Pusch (Ed.), *Multicultural education: A cross-cultural training approach.* Yarmouth, ME: Intercultural Press.

iEARN. (n.d.). Learning circles: Teachers' guide (www.iearn.org/circles/lcguide/) Internet 2 K–20 Initiative, Muse. Retrieved August 25, 2008, from http://k20.internet2.edu/getstarted/k-12

International Society for Technology in Education (ISTE). (2007). *National educational technology standards for students* (2nd ed.). Eugene, OR: ISTE.

Kirkwood, T. (2001). Our global age requires global education: Clarifying definitional ambiguities. *Social Studies, 92,* 1–16.

Kniep, W. (1987). *Next steps in global education: A handbook for curriculum development.* NY: American Forum for Global Education.

Ladson-Billings, G. (2005). Differing concepts of citizenship: Schools and communities as sites of civic development. In N. Noddings (Ed.), *Educating citizens for global awareness (p. 73).* New York: Columbia University, Teachers' College Press.

Le Roux, J. (2001). Re-examining global education's relevance beyond 2000. *Research in Education, 65,* 70–80. Retrieved from http://journals.mup.man.ac.uk/cgi-bin/pdfdisp/MUPpdf/RED/V65I0/650070.pdf

Lenhart, A., & Madden M. (2005). Pew Internet & American Life Project, *Teen Content Creators and Consumers,* 1.

Lenhart A., & Madden, M., (2007). Pew Internet & American Life Project, Teens, Privacy and Online Social Networks.

Lindsay, J. (2007). Flat Classroom Project and New Ways of Learning. Retrieved August 26, 2008, from http://julielindsay.tigblog.org/post/194663

Lindsay, J. (2006). Julie Lindsay's Presentation Links/Podcasting in the Classroom. Retrieved August 26, 2008, from http://julielindsaylinks.pbwiki.com/Podcasting+in+the+Classroom#WhyPodcasting

Mathews, J. T. (1997). Power shift. *Foreign Affairs,* January/February, 50–66. Retrieved August 25, 2008, from www.fpvmv.umb.sk/fpvmv_www/phprs/storage/File/ksp/GLUN/S_Matthews_FA.pdf

Meagher, J. (2007). Survivor Gault Canada. TakingITGlobal. Retrieved August 25, 2008, from www.takingitglobal.org/tiged/bp/contents/001.html. Now available at http://tig.phpwebhosting.com/tiged/TIGed-MTC.pdf; or at www.tig.org/bestpractices (pages 10–11).

Merryfield, M. (Ed). (1997). *Preparing teachers to teach global perspectives: A handbook for teacher educators.* Thousand Oaks, CA: Corwin Press.

Merryfield, M. (2002). The difference a global educator can make. *Educational Leadership, 60*(2), 18–21.

Mid-continent Research for Education and Learning, *Content Knowledge* (4th ed.). Retrieved April 29, 2009 from www.mcrel.org/compendium/browse.asp

National Academy of Sciences Center for Science, Mathematics, and Engineering Education. (1996). National science education standards. Washington, DC: National Academies Press. Retrieved August 26, 2008, from www.nap.edu/html/nses/6d.html

November, A. (2007). November Learning 6 (June). Retrieved August 25, 2008, from http://novemberlearning.com/index.php?option=com_content&task=view&id=105&Itemid=95

Nussbaum, M. (1994). Patriotism and cosmopolitanism. *The Boston Review 19*(5). Retrieved from www.bsos.umd.edu/gvpt/Theory/Patriotism and Cosmopolitanism.pdf

Partnership for 21st Century Skills. (2008). Tucson, AZ: www.21stcenturyskills.org. Retrieved from www.21stcenturyskills.org/documents/p21_wi2008.pdf

Pedagogical Advisory Group (Galvin, C., Gilleran, A., Hogenbirk, P., Hunya, M., Selinger, M., & Zeidler, B.). (September 2006). Reflections on eTwinning: Collaboration and eTwinning, enrichment and added value of eTwinning projects. Retrieved from www.etwinning.net/shared/data/etwinning/general/pag_i.pdf

Peters, L. (2007). Meeting the needs of the vulnerable learner: The role of the teacher in bridging the gap between informal and formal learning using digital technologies. In T. Willoughby & E. Wood (Eds.), *Children's learning in a digital world.* Hoboken, NJ: Wiley-Blackwell.

Piaget, J. (1993). Johann Amos Comenius. Prospects, 23 (1/2), 173–196. Geneva: UNESCO, International Bureau of Education. Retrieved from www.ibe.unesco.org/fileadmin/user_upload/archive/publications/ThinkersPdf/comeniuse.pdf

Pike, G., & Selby, D. (1988). *Global teacher, global learner.* London: Hodder and Stoughton & York, UK: The Centre for Global Education, York University.

Pink, D. (2005). *A whole new mind: Moving from the information age to the conceptual age.* New York: Riverhead Books.

Plutarch. (n.d.). *On the fortune of Alexander.* Quoted in M. Nussbaum. (1994). Patriotism and cosmopolitanism. From *The Boston Review, 19*(5). Retrieved from www.bsos.umd.edu/gvpt/Theory/Patriotism and Cosmopolitanism.pdf

Prensky, M. (2005). Engage me or enrage me: What today's learners demand. *EDUCAUSE Review, 40*(5), 60–65. Retrieved August 25, 2008, from http://connect.educause.edu/Library/EDUCAUSE+Review/EngageMeorEnrageMe WhatTod/40579

Richardson, W. (2006). *Blogs, wikis, podcasts, and other powerful web tools for classrooms.* Thousand Oaks, CA: Corwin Press/SAGE Publications.

Riel, M. [1997] (2006). *Learning circles: Teachers' guide.* Retrieved from www.iearn.org/circles/lcguide

Rogers, A. (1999, February). The origins of a global learning network. Retrieved from http://gsh.lightspan.com/gsh/teach/articles/origins.htm

Salmon Bay School. Eating Local. Retrieved April 29, 2008, from http://bridgesweb.org/project_videos/Seattle/seattle_200708/projSea_localfood.html

Schwartz, L., Clark, S., Cossarin, M., & Rudolph, J. (2004). Educational wikis: Features and selection criteria. *International Review of Research in Open and Distance Learning, 5*(1). Retrieved August 26, 2008, from www.irrodl.org/index.php/irrodl/article/view/163/692

Seneca. (n.d.). *De Otio*. Quoted in M. Nussbaum. (1994). Patriotism and cosmopolitanism. From *The Boston Review, 19*(5). Retrieved from www.bsos.umd.edu/gvpt/Theory/Patriotism and Cosmopolitanism.pdf

Shrock, Kathy. (1999–2009). Kathy Schrock's guide for educators. Discovery Education. Retrieved August 26, 2008, from http://school.discoveryeducation.com/schrockguide/edtools.html

Smith, M. W., & Wilhelm, J. D. (2002). *Reading don't fix no Chevys: Literacy in the lives of young men*. Portsmouth, NH: Heinemann.

Stanzler, J. (n.d.). The Arab-Israeli conflict. Interactive Communications & Simulations at the University of Michigan-Flint and Ann Arbor. Retrieved August 25, 2008, from http://ics.soe.umich.edu/main/section/2

Stewart, V. (2007). Becoming citizens of the world. *Educational Leadership, 64*(7), 8–14. Retrieved August 26, 2008, from www.ascd.org/authors/ed_lead/el200704_stewart.html; available at http://worldroom.tamu.edu/Blog/Text/May21/Becoming-Citizens-of-the-World.pdf

Survivor Gault. Taking ITGLOBAL. Retrieved August 25, 2008 from www.takingitglobal.org/tiged/bp/contents/001.html

Tapscott, D., & Williams, A. (2006). *Wikinomics—How mass collaboration changes everything*. New York: Portfolio.

TESAN: The Endangered Species and Nature of the World. Available from www.tesan.vuurwerk.nl

Tye, K. A. (2003). Globalizing global education to nurture world citizens. *Education Digest 69*(4), 18–23.

Tye, K. A., & Tye, B. B. (1993). The realities of schooling: Overcoming teacher resistance to global education. *Theory into Practice, 32*(1), 58–63.

United Nations Educational, Scientific, and Cultural Organization (UNESCO). (2003). Report of the global review of the UNESCO association schools project: Results, recommendations and conclusions. Review conducted by the Centre for International Education and Research, University of Birmingham, UK. Available at http://portal.unesco.org/education/en/files/23509/10654517241Global_Review_Report_ENG.pdf/Global+Review+Report+ENG.pdf

Index

1001 Flat World Tales, 51, 74, 137
30 Boxes, 138

A

accountability pressures, 36–37
Ahmed, Akbar, 100
alternatives, knowledge of, 82, 84–85
American Forum for Global Education, 133
Amnesty International, 95, 130, 135
analyzing project information, 58–59
Animal Diaries project, 32, 135
Animoto, 88, 135
Antarctica, project on, 78, 138
Asia Society, 133
assessment design, 88
Associated Schools Project Network, 130
asynchronous communication, 119, 121
"An Attainable Global Perspective" (essay), 81
awareness, cross-cultural, 82, 83–84, 91
awareness, global, 120
    in curriculum objectives, 36
    for elementary school students, 91–93
Ayiti: The Cost of Life, 52–53

B

Babelfish, 135
Baltic Sea Project, 127
Bennett, Judith, 31
Bennett, Milton, 12
Bishop, Bill, 100
Blogger.com, 135
blogging
    defined, 119
    Flat Classroom project, 40–41
    Ning social network tool vs., 42
    self-reflection blogs, 87
blogs, 14
Books Go Global! project, 74
Brazilian rainforest, project on, 77
Brown, Seeley, 10
Buddy Project (Indiana), 31
Burrell, Clay, 98
business changes, 99

C

calendar, shared, 14
The California Arts Project (TCAP), 136
California Telemation Project, 119
Carvin, Andy, 17, 18–19
case studies
    early experiences (Cheryl Vitali), 25–26
    Globaldreamers (Marsha Goren), 24–25
    Kim Cofino, interview with, 72–76
    mentoring and collaboration (Joan Goble), 31–33

Center for Global Involvement Education, 127
Center for Teaching International Relations (CTIR), 134
Chinese American International School (CAIS), 100
choices, awareness of, 82, 84–85
Choices Education Program, 134
CIA World Factbook, 87, 136
Cinderella Around the World (lesson), 103–106
City Quest, 136
City Quest projects, 32
classroom, global, 49–50
CNN Student News, 94, 130, 136
Cofino, Kim, 72–76
collaboration. See also global education networks; social networking
    advice on. See getting started
    iEARN. See iEARN network
    introducing students to, 50
    and lesson planning, 33–34
    NETS•S standard for, 44, 140
    Ning for. See Ning social network tool
    power of (case study), 31–33
    preparing for, 85–86
    projects. See starting projects
    Web 2.0 as opportunity for, 11, 13
collaborative projects. See projects
Colorful Classrooms project, 70
Comenius, Johann Amos, 17
Comenius Project, 78
communication
    advice and pitfalls, 76
    NETS•S standard for, 44, 140
    synchronous, preparing for, 85

competitive students, Web resources for, 125–126
Connected Classroom: Social Networking via Ning project, 74
consciousness, perspective, 82, 82–83
content sharing tools, 88
Cooperative Education Movement, 57
Copen, Peter, 59–60, 63
cosmopolitanism, 12–13
Council of Chief State School Officers, 35
country research, 87
CountryWatch, 87, 136
Coverdell World Wise Schools program, 128
"Creating a Global Difference: Conversations for 21st Century Teachers" (video), 8
cross-cultural awareness, 82, 83–84, 91
Cross-Cultural Pen Pals (lesson), 115–118
Cubberley, Ellwood P., 28–29
cultural exchanges, 21
    cross-cultural awareness, 82, 83–84
    defined, 119
    global dynamics (interconnectedness), 82, 84
current events activities, 93–95
curriculum objectives, 14–15
    collaboration and lesson planning, 33–34
    Flat Classroom project, 43
    global awareness with, 36
    integrating global perspectives into, 81–89
    sample module design, 87
Cyber UN Schoolbus, 130

D

Daniel, René, 57
Davis, Vicki, 39, 40. See also Flat Classroom project
    on launching global classrooms, 49
De Orilla a Orilla project, 62
de Vries, Rene, 26, 31, 33
democratic thinking, 28
Design and Technical Quality (NETS criterion)
    Flat Classroom project, 45
desire for social justice, 21–22, 27–28
Dewey, John, 28–29
Dietz, Karrie, 27, 30, 34
digital citizenship, 141, 147
digital identities, 119
digital immigrants, 119
digital natives, 9, 119
digital stories, 40, 44–50, 119
Digital Storyteller, 14, 136
Digiteen Project, 48
dimensions for global perspectives, 81–82
Diogenes, 12
DiScipio, Tim, 70
Discovery Channel, 76
Discovery Education, 136
diversity
    increased, U.S., 1–2
    UNESCO Universal Declaration on Cultural Diversity, 7
Do Food Choices Affect Global Warming (lesson), 107–114
Doors to Diplomacy site, 125
Dubos, René, 35
dynamics, global, 82, 84

E

Earth Force, 134
educational networking, 57. See also iEARN network
educators, 98
    ELL teachers, 29
    finding partner teachers, 85, 129–130
    global educators, about, 98, 120
Eduspaces, 136
elementary school students, activity for, 91–93
ELL teachers, 29
empathy for others, 21, 22–23
engagement, new paths for, 21, 23
enrichment, new paths for, 21, 23
ePals, 70–72, 136
    activity for elementary students (example), 91–93
    bulletin boards for partner teachers, 85
ePals School Blog, 136
Erasmus, Desiderius, 16
e-Twinning site, 79
European Schoolnet, 136
evaluating
    global education technical projects, 74
    iEARN network, 63–65
Evanston Township High School (Illinois), 100
Evoka, 136

F

Facebook, 136
fairy tales lesson (example), 103–106
Feeding Minds (Fighting Hunger), 63, 64, 136
file sharing, defined, 120

Index

finding new ways to enrich and engage, 21, 23
Flat Classroom project, 39–54, 86, 136
    blogging, 40–41
    NETS standards with project outcome, 43
    Ning social network tool, 42
    podcasts and vodcasts, 41
    projects inspired from, 50–54
    screenshots of, 43, 45–49
    Skype, 41
Flat Stanley, 126
Flickr, 88, 136
formatting lessons, 86
Free Educational Mail (FrEdMail) Network. See Global Schoolhouse
Freinet, Célestin, 56, 57–59
Friedman, Thomas, 39. See also Flat Classroom project
Friends and Flags program, 24–25, 136
FTP, defined, 120

G

Gardner, Howard, 2
George Soros Open Society Institute, 60
Gersh, Susan, 72
GET (Global Educators Team), 33
getting started, 13–14
    advice and pitfalls, 75–76
    preparation as essential, 85–86
    on projects. See starting projects
    quick-start project examples, 91–95
Global Academies, 120
global awareness, 120
    in curriculum objectives, 36
    for elementary school students, 91–93

Global Classrooms, 85
global classrooms, launching, 49–50
Global Climate Change, 131
global collaboration. See collaboration
global dynamics, knowledge of, 82, 84
global education (in general)
    accountability pressures and, 36–37
    advice on. See getting started
    coinage of term, 35
    curriculum of, 14
    defining, 5–6
    educator Kim Cofino on, 72–76
    origins of, 12–13
    projects. See projects
    21st-century skills, 35–36
Global Education Motivators, 129
global education networks
    Comenius Project, 78
    ePals. See ePals
    e-Twinning site, 79
    Global Schoolhouse, 67–70, 85, 136
    Jason Project, 77
    Live from Antarctica project, 78
    Passport to Knowledge project, 77
    Science across the World project, 76–77, 138
    Taking IT Global, 77, 78
Global Gateway, 129
Global Kids' Digital Media Initiative, 51, 52–54
Global Kids Project, 136
Global Kidz, 136
Global Learning and Observations to Benefit the Environment (GLOBE), 134–135
Global Learning Communities, 129

global literacy, 99
Global Nomads Group (GNG), 27–28, 93–94, 136
global perspectives
    defined, 120
    five dimensions for, 81–82
Global Schoolhouse (GSN), 67–70, 136
    bulletin boards for partner teachers, 85
    example project, 69
Global Schoolnet, 136
global themes, integrating into curriculum, 81–89
    dimensions for global perspectives, 81–82
    preparation as essential, 85–86
    sample module design, 87–89
global warming lesson (example), 107–114
Global Youth Voices, 136
Globaldreamers, 24–25
GlobalEd project, 127
globalization, 97–98
Globe community, 128
Goble, Joan, 26, 29–30, 31–33, 34
Google Earth, 87, 136
Google Groups, 136
Google News, 136
Goren, Marsha, 23, 24–25
Gragert, Ed, 60-61
The Green Wave project, 70
GSN. See Global Schoolhouse

H

Haiti family project, 52–53
Hanvey, Robert, 81
homogeneous communities, 100
Horizon Project, 50, 136

human choices, awareness of, 82, 84–85
Hunt, James B., Jr., 98

I

iEarn, 137
iEARN network, 55–65
    bulletin boards for partner teachers, 85
    De Orilla a Orilla project, 62
    evaluating, 63–65
    Feeding Minds Fighting Hunger project, 63, 64
    founding and expansion, 59–61
    Global Schoolhouse vs., 70
    homepage, 56
instant messaging, defined, 120
interconnectedness, global cultural, 82, 84
International Baccalaureate Organisation (IBO), 133
International Education and Resource Network. See iEARN network
"international education" term, 21, 34. See also global education (in general)
introductory profiles, 87
Irving, John, 70

J

Jason Project, 77, 137
justice, social, 21–22, 27–28

K

Kidlink, 85, 135, 137
KidProj, 127
Kindergarten Connections: Connecting Students via VoiceThread project, 73
knowledge of alternatives, 82, 84–85
knowledge of global dynamics, 82, 84
knowledge of world conditions, 82, 83
kosmu polites, 12

L

La Coopérative de L'Enseignement Laïc, 57
Labelle, Linda, 93
Lambert, Ann, 22–23, 85
language translation tools, 11
Learning Circles format, 58
learning theory, 10–11
lesson planning. See also curriculum objectives
    collaboration and, 33–34
    finding student passions, 95
    preparing work with partner teachers, 85–86
    sample (ePals), 72
    sample module design, 87
    Web resources for, 130–132
lesson plans (examples)
    Cinderella Around the World, 103–106
    Cross-Cultural Pen Pals, 115–118
    Do Food Choices Affect Global Warming, 107–114
    Web resources for, 128–129
Lindsay, Julie, 39, 41, 49. See also Flat Classroom project
literacy, global, 99
Live from Antarctica project, 78
Lodi, Mario, 57

M

Map Machine (National Geographic), 87, 137
mapping, 87
mathematics
    Mathlincs project, 50–51, 137
    standards for, global awareness with, 36
Mathlincs, 50–51, 137

McAulliffe, Sherry, 22
Meaning of Friendship: Students as Authors via SmartBoards project, 73
mentoring, 29–33
Merryfield, Merry M., 98
Metni, Eliane, 27
middle school students, activities for, 93–95
middle school students, activity of, 93–95
Mills, Steve, 99
Model United Nations Headquarters, 135
module design (sample), 87–89
monocultural, defined, 120
multimedia tools, 14, 88
music, global, 95
My Hero, 137
MySpace, 9, 137

N

NASA Education, 137
NASA's Jason Project, 77, 137
NASA's Live from Antarctica project, 78
NASA's Passport to Knowledge project, 77
National Educational Technology Standards. See NETS
National Geographic's Map Machine, 87, 137
National Geographic's Xpeditions, 128
National Public Radio (NPR), 137
NETS (National Educational Technology Standards), 139–147
    for Administrators (NETS•A), 145–147
    Flat Classroom project, 43
    for Students (NETS•S), 36, 139–141
    communication and collaboration, 44
    global elements of, 36
    for Teachers (NETS•T), 142–144

networks. See global education networks; social networking

New York Times, 131

news-based activities, 93–95

Newseum, 94, 131, 137

9/11, events of, 4, 61

Ning social network tool
- Connected Classroom project, 74
- defined, 120
- Flat Classroom project, 42, 46–49
- introducing students to, 49–50
- World Village project, 74

NOAA (National Oceanic & Atmospheric Administration) Education, 137

Nussbaum, Martha, 12–13

O

objectives. See curriculum objectives

ocean floor, project on, 77

1001 Flat World Tales, 51, 74, 137

OneTrueMedia service, 88, 137

online communities. See social networking

Online Engagement and Interaction with the Project (NETS criterion)
- Flat Classroom project, 47

Orillas. See De Orilla a Orilla project

Oxfam website, 95, 128, 131–132, 137

P

pansophism, 17

partner teacher, finding, 85, 129–130

Partnership for 21st-Century Skills, 35, 99

Passport to Antarctica project, 137

Passport to Knowledge project, 77, 138

pathways to global education, 21–37
- accountability pressures, 36–37
- collaboration and lesson planning, 33–34
- desire for social justice, 21–22, 27–28
- empathy for others, 21, 22–23
- new ways to enrich and engage, 21, 23
- support and mentoring, 29–33

PBS (Public Broadcasting Service), 76, 132

PBS Wide Angle, 132

Peace Corps, 132

pen pals. See ePals

perspective consciousness, 82, 82–83

perspectives, global
- defined, 120
- five dimensions for, 81–82

Phi Delta Kappan Resource Guide, 133

pitfalls with globally collaborative projects, 13–14
- advice and pitfalls, 75–76
- opportunities with Web 2.0, 13–14
- preparation as essential, 85–86
- quick-start examples, 91–95

Plutte, Chris, 27

podcasts
- defined, 121
- Flat Classroom project, 41

preparation as essential, 85–86

profiles of students, 87

project information, analyzing, 58–59

projects. See also specific project by name
- analyzing project information, 58–59
- integrating global themes, 81–89
- objectives. See curriculum objectives
- quick-start examples, 91–95
- starting. See starting projects
- technical, list of, 72–76

Public Educators' Co-operative, 57
Public Broadcasting Service (PBS), 76, 132

R
Race to the Bottom, 54
rainforest, project on, 77
Reflection and Evaluation (NETS criterion)
    Flat Classroom project, 47
reflective blogs, defined, 121
Riel, Margaret, 58
Rogers, Al, 58
RSS feeds, defined, 121
Rubistar, 137

S
sample module design, 87–89
scaffolding, defined, 121
school partnering services, 129–130
SchoolNet Africa, 130
Science across the World project, 76–77, 137
science standards (U.S.), 36
ScrapBlog, 88, 137
Screencast-O-Matic, 137
screencasts, 121
Second Life, 51–52, 137
security considerations, 17–19
self-reflection blogs, 87
September 11 (2001), events of, 4, 61
Shrock, Kathy, 15
simulations, 51–54
Skype, 138
    defined, 121
    Flat Classroom project, 41
    introducing students to, 49–50
Small Moments: ESL Students Present via VoiceThread project, 74

social demands of Web 2.0 tools, 49
social justice, desire for, 21–22, 27–28
social learning, 10–11, 121
social networking, 9–11, 76. See also Ning social network tool
    Connected Classroom project, 74
    defined, 121
    ePals. See ePals
    introducing students to, 50
South Pole, project about, 78
standards, global perspective and, 36–37
starting projects, 13–14
    advice and pitfalls, 75–76
    opportunities with Web 2.0, 13–14
    preparation as essential, 85–86
    quick-start examples, 91–95
state-of-the-planet awareness, 82, 83
Stoics, 12
storyboarding, 40, 121
student profiles, 87
student writing, editing, 59
students, Web resources for, 125–138
support, 29–30
surface layer (of people), 81
Survey Monkey, 138
synchronous communications
    defined, 121
    preparing for, 85
Synthesis and Construction of Ideas (NETS criterion)
    Flat Classroom project, 46

T
Taking IT Global, 76–77, 78, 138
Tapscott, Donald, 99
teachers. See educators

Teacher's Guide to International Collaboration, 128–129
technology
    business changes, 99
    content sharing tools, 88
    cross-cultural awareness and, 83–84
    demands of Web 2.0 tools, 49
    knowledge of alternatives and, 84–85
    knowledge of global dynamics and, 84
    knowledge of world conditions and, 83
    list of technical projects, 72–76
    perspective consciousness and, 83
Teen Second Life, 52–54, 138
Telecollaborate! website, 133
TENAN (The Endangered Animals of the World), 32
TESAN (The Endangered Species and Nature of the World), 32
ThinkQuest, 126
ThinkQuest Competition, 125
30Boxes, 14, 138
1001 Flat World Tales, 51, 74, 137
tools, list of (free), 15
traditional classrooms, Web-2.0 equivalents, 10–11
translation tools, 11
Travel Buddies, 138
Trees and Forests project (Elanora Heights Primary School), 31–32
"21st-century skills" term, 35

U

UNESCO (United Nations Educational, Scientific and Cultural Organization), 76
UNESCO Universal Declaration on Cultural Diversity, 7

UNICEF (United Nations Children's Fund), 76, 138

V

video (companion to this book), 8
videoconferencing, 121. See also Skype
virtual meetings, 85, 121
virtual reality, 51, 122
Virtual Tour activity, 93
Vitali, Cheryl, 25–26, 33
vlogs, defined, 122
vodcasts
    defined, 122
    Flat Classroom project, 41
Voice over Internet Protocol (VoIP), defined, 122. See also Skype
Voices of Youth (UNICEF), 138
VoiceThread, 88, 138
    defined, 122
    projects with, list of, 73–74

W

warm-up activities, 87
Web 2.0, 9–19
    curriculum objectives and, 14–15
    defined, 122
    demands of, understanding, 49
    free tools, list of, 15
    getting started, 13–14
    learning theory, 10–11
    as opportunity for collaboration, 11, 13
    preparing work with partner teachers, 85
    security considerations, 17–19
Web resources, list of, 125–138
webinars, defined, 122
WebQuest, defined, 122

Index

The WIDE ANGLE Global Classroom, 132
widgets, defined, 122
wikis, 14, 39, 88. See also Flat Classroom project
  defined, 122
  introducing students to, 49–50
  Ning social network tool vs., 42
  preparing for global collaboration, 85–86
Wikispaces, 138
Williams, Anthony, 99
Windows Movie Maker, 122, 138
world citizens, 12–13
world conditions, knowledge of, 82, 83
world hunger project, iEARN, 63

World Village project, 74
Worldbank You Think Issues, 138
worldviews, recognition of different, 82–83
writing (student), editing, 59

X

Xpeditions (National Geographic), 128

Y

younger students, Web resources for, 126–127
Youth Voices, 138
"Youth Window" (Feeding Minds Fighting Hunger), 63
YouTube, 9, 138